The Preaching Ministry

The Preaching Ministry

by
James B. Chapman

A PALCON Reprint

Beacon Hill Press of Kansas City
Kansas City, Missouri

First Printing, 1947
Revised Edition (PALCON), 1976

ISBN: 0-8341-0446-6

Printed in the
United States of America

Contents

Foreword

It seems most appropriate to bring Dr. Chapman's outstanding contribution of *The Preaching Ministry* back into circulation for PALCON. This book was for many years a standard work in the Church of the Nazarene in the course of study for ministerial students, in both the home study and college programs.

To those who heard the lecture series at the Nazarene Theological Seminary, it will revive a wonderful memory. To the hundreds who will read it in this new edition it will represent a voice from the past leadership of our beloved Zion with a timeless and relevant message to the ministry of our day.

—Charles H. Strickland
General Superintendent

Preface

To those who listened to these lectures when they were given as the Basil Miller series in the Nazarene Theological Seminary in January, 1947, I feel a debt of thanksgiving. To those who take the time to read, now that the material is presented in book form, I address a special request for charity and consideration.

At the very most, I can hope that the things we have sought to emphasize here may merit the further consideration of those who recognize preaching as their vocation in life; for it will be that further consideration that will net the real profit. I have sought to present only things that are fundamental, and I believe the mere lifting up of these essentials may serve a good purpose in the lives of preaching men and women; and to these I would offer the apostolic invitation, "Think on these things."

No lecture or book can be expected to make anyone over. I shall be content if, when the reports are all in, it is found that what I have said or written has served to help some servant of Jesus Christ serve just a little more effectively than he otherwise would have done.

To all who preach the good gospel of Jesus Christ, I would offer the goal of being good preachers. I would not measure by the standard of others, but would for each one make the standard that better preacher who in both your dreams and waking hours beckons you on.

—James B. Chapman

1

Substantial Preaching Demanded

A prospective missionary, describing the ground of his conviction that he was called to be a missionary, told how in both visions and in dreams he saw himself standing before the people of the land toward which he had now set his face, preaching the gospel to them. He was aware that there is much to do besides preaching, but it was this vision of preaching that made all the rest take on meaning. I think it was that way with us all, and that it will continue to be that way through life. The minister's life involves many things: pastoral work, administrative work, and work of undefined character. But that which lifts all these activities from the plane of drudgery is the prospect and possibility of standing up to deliver the message of Christ in the unction of the Spirit. One can do the other things, even the most undesirable and monotonous of them, if by so doing he can purchase a chance to preach.

I do not in this instance speak of pleasure in any ordinary sense, and yet I think God does so assure the hearts of His anointed ones that they can come to the time for preaching clothed in a garment of joy and praise. They can come to Sunday morning, saying in their hearts, "This is the day the Lord hath made. Let us rejoice in it and be glad." Those who tell of their dread of preaching (Spurgeon said his knees always knocked when he stood up to preach) are but coming to the subject from another approach. There is a sense of responsibility that is challenging, and without this no one can know the joy of preaching. But this dread is like the hunger that is forgotten when the soul is filled.

In a denominational journal there recently appeared an article under the title "When Is the Preacher Worth His Salt?" The answer to the titular question is quite carefully concealed beneath many deserved complaints against those who cumber the holy office; but the answer is there in strong words: "The preacher is God's vice-regent, deputed by divine authority to exercise a holy commission. He is Christ's ambassador, entrusted with all the negotiations involved in winning lost men and a belligerent world." The writer quotes a prominent columnist as saying of the ministry:

> Men to match this hour are tragically lacking. Especially regrettable is the lack of great preachers. They are the ones to whom we nat-

urally look for spiritual leadership, but too many of them are uninspired men merely holding jobs. The prophet note is not heard in their pulpits, nor leadership felt in their congregations.

Rev. Armacost, the author of "When Is the Preacher Worth His Salt?" in a notable paragraph says:

> A minister is a prophet of God. He is under orders. If no agonizing, terrifying convictions impelled him to enter this holy office, he had better never touch it.

And farther along he says:

> The preacher has allowed the old techniques and dynamics of the camp meeting, the revival, the sawdust trail, the prayer meeting, and, pretty largely, the Sunday evening services to go into the discard, and has relaxed with a sigh of relief. But he has not, through travail of soul, brought forth with daring adventure any modern equivalent in improved techniques. Instead he has buried those result-producing methods in graves of oblivion, and goes tiptoeing among the tombstones as though he feared some of them might come to life again to plague him.

To be at his best, a workman should be ashamed neither of himself nor of his calling. But if shame must attach, it is better that he should be a mediocre workman in a worthy field than that he should be accomplished in a calling of no consequence. This is no place for a eulogy on the ministry as a calling. We are at this moment more concerned with facts as they are, with reference to this work, than we are with ideals of what should be. By this I mean that we are not going to work under ideal conditions, but under real conditions, conditions largely ready-made for us by others.

When Paul talked of "the foolishness of preaching," he may have been reflecting estimates picked up from his contemporaries. On Mars' hill, you know, the wise men called Paul "a babbler," and this and similar words may have been used of preachers more than the written records show. By using the phrase "foolishness of preaching" in the connection that he did, Paul tacitly admitted his own inability to defend the adequacy of such means to the end toward which it was directed. There is no task so monumental as that involved in saving men from sin, making good men out of bad, and that this should be accomplished by simply preaching to them rather than by applying force of a more tangible sort, is positing an effect without proscribing a sufficient cause, according to the judgment of the great majority of the world of mankind. This discrepancy must have been apparent to the Greeks, as it has been to thinking people ever since, even including those whose lives are devoted to the sacred task of preaching.

So bent are men of all callings to find excuses for their shortcomings that they ride exhausted hobbies even after they are dead. For example, it is common in our times to hear people, and especially preachers, condemn our day as being irreverent and unsympathetic toward preachers. But if one reads of Paul's humiliating experiences at the hands of popular mobs, by order of civil authorities, and by urge of rival religious leaders, he will marvel that Paul's ministerial dignity could be maintained. Or if one takes the stonings and mockings which John Wesley and his coadjutors endured, he may wonder that the preacher of the present day is given such a pedestal on which to stand. Men have not usually thought of their day as favorable. It is always some day of the past, or, in rare instances of proper facing, some day in the future that is happy. Today is too real to be ideal, and bargain seekers find the price of alibis favor the selection of "the times" as a good buy. But for practical purposes we may dispose of this whole matter by saying simply that our day is what it is, and that it is a challenge for us to meet it. If we ever make good at all we shall have to do it during our own day and generation—other days must be left with the fathers or committed to the sons.

There is no calling in which the current element is stronger than in the calling of the minister. His message is unchanging, but his methods must be ever changing. When men have tampered with the message in the endeavor to adapt it to their times, they have erred destructively, whether they have gone to the right, toward compromise, or to the left, toward fanaticism and cultism. But when men have held fast to methods because of their inability to discern between message and methods, they have erred in effectiveness and have failed in their task.

We of today must give to men the same message given by our Master, but we must adapt our methods to many situations that did not exist in Palestine when He "spake as never man spake" in the preaching of His own glorious gospel. The same may be said of all the generations since, leading up to our own. We cannot follow the sermon forms that were so effective in the preaching of John Wesley. We cannot preach so long at one time as did Charles G. Finney. Camp meetings are neither so unusual nor so effective as they were in the days of Inskip and MacDonald. There were factors in the ministry of Drs. Bresee and Walker that do not find answer in the situations of today. Even methods we ourselves followed yesterday must be modified to fit today and the clost tomorrow. All these things are valid and challenging. The ministry is no place for mossbacks who insist on using a rock in one end of the corn sack to balance against the corn in the other end, just because their fathers did it that way; it is no place for Rip Van Winkles who sleep for 20 years while the world goes on to a new day. The ministry as a calling is everything but monotonous, for it is ever challenging and ever new.

The basic error is that of supposing that because the demands now are different as regarding the methods of preaching, they are therefore either less or, as some would pessimistically hold, nonexistent. We lay it down as the center of our present thesis that our day demands substantial preaching. When we say it demands it, we mean both that it needs it and that it calls for it.

1. The Church Itself Demands Substantial Preaching

Dr. Donald S. Metz, in an article recently submitted to the *Preacher's Magazine*, says:

> A free or informal church makes demands upon its ministers far greater than does the formal or liturgical church. The more formal a church becomes, the more the minister becomes a priest—the spokesman of the church. The less formal a church is, the more the minister becomes a prophet—the spokesman of God.

If, then, the tendency is for churches to become more liturgical, no matter whether we are speaking of denominations or of local churches within denominations, the tendency is to make less of preaching and more of other forms of ministerial service. This tendency may be the result of the preacher's inability or unwillingness to preach. But in a service that is climaxed by the sermon, a weak sermon means a weak service. As Dr. Metz says, "The liturgical service is alter-centered, while the informal service is pulpit-centered." Hence, as might be expected, liturgical churches do not produce outstanding preachers, and strong preachers do not develop liturgical churches. Since most people, including preachers, are inclined to "take the way of least resistance," a saying which traced, to its basis, means that most people are temperamentally lazy and try to get along without hard work, and since it is easier to plan a good liturgical service than to prepare to preach well, the preachers make the formal service their refuge, and the people accept a good service in the place of a good sermon which they would not get anyway.

It is not within the scope of the present assignment to discuss the general scope of the minister's task, nor yet to enter into the subject of the worship service—having set our own limits within the bounds of the preaching section. Our reference to the worship service is not a criticism but rather a warning. The alternates are not, as I believe, between a good worship service with poor preaching and a poor worship service with good preaching. The real choice should be something better than either of these; namely, a good worship service with good preaching.

Neither is it within the scope of our present purpose to speak of the multitudinous activities connected with the preacher's calling, even though by these the preacher buys his opportunity to preach. It has never been possible to separate the pastor and the preacher. No matter how large the church, the man that preaches is the pastor in the thinking of the people, and if the man that calls does not preach when the people return the call, they feel that it is an off day in the church. And here, again, we would not mention to berate but to warn. The tendency to compensate is so ingrained in us that candid people have learned to think of a good pastor as a poor preacher, and of a good preacher as a careless or untactful pastor. But it need not and should not be so. It should be the determination of every minister to be as balanced and complete as time and ability permit.

It has been difficult for people to quote that scriptural passage on the relationship of priest and people. Some quote it, "like priest, like people," and some say, "Like people, like priest." But the fact is that both orders have been observed. Churches tend to produce preachers to their liking, and preachers tend to force churches into their own mold. In some instances the churches are within their rights, and in others the preachers must set, not follow, the fashions.

But you of this seminary are in training for service in churches that require prophets, speaking for God, more than priests, speaking for the church. The churches you will serve want preaching preachers, and the fact that you are here indicates that you want to be preaching preachers. But even in our group, there are plenty of instances in which preaching is relegated to a secondary, even to a minor place, by reason of so many and such extended activities. We are not, as a rule, long on ritual, but we are long on announcements, special singing, collections, and the introductions of friends and strangers. So that the "after which the preacher will preach" (of which General Superintendent Williams used to speak so tellingly) often comes just 10 minutes before time for the benediction.

But I believe these monstrosities which pass

for religious meetings are either made or permitted by the preacher in charge, and are not on the demand or by the wish of the spiritual section of the church. If these things do represent the desires of the church, the church is mistaken and the preacher should tactfully correct it. If the church wants substantial preaching, it must make place for it. In the sphere of the natural, it is sometimes necessary to create a demand for that which is needed and available. When bananas appeared on the market a few years ago, the public had no appetite for them. Yet bananas are a good and useful food and are abundantly available, so interested persons set in systematically to create a desire and appetite for bananas, and with what success we are all witnesses. If this can be done on the markets of this world, it can be done also regarding good preaching, and it must be done if the Protestant church is to prosper and continue to grow. For whenever substantial preaching gives way to liturgy, the influence of the Protestant church takes second place to the Roman Catholic, for as a liturgical institution, no body of people can successfully compete with the Roman Catholic church. Men can follow the liturgy blindly, but Protestant Christianity must have an informed constituency; and, with all the various methods in vogue for promoting Christian education, the historic method of teaching by preaching still retains its preeminence. Truth is not gospel truth until it is presented by Spirit-anointed preachers. Classrooms and lecture halls may teach Bible history and geography and make people wise concerning philosophical and logical truths. But that gospel which is the power of God unto salvation cannot be read out of a book, lifted from a picture on page or screen, heard on phonograph or radio, but must be preached by living men to living men.

I talked with Bishop Pickett in India regarding mission methods. The bishop said, "There is no way of founding the church anywhere except the way of Jesus and the apostles—just by preaching the gospel. It never has worked when people have built church buildings as a means of founding the church, or have established hospitals or schools for the same purpose. The order is and always has been, to preach the gospel until the people are saved, then build buildings in which they can worship, and establish hospitals for the curing of their bodies, and schools for the education of the minds."

I would add to the bishop's observation this one word more: God's method of preserving the purity and power of His Church is distinctly connected with the preaching of the gospel; and every other way, when it becomes a substitute for substantial preaching, results in spiritual deterioration and essential defeat. If the Church is to continue to be the Church, the chief place must be given to preaching the gospel in the hearing of the people who constitute the Church. So that, in truth, the Church cannot be either brought into being or preserved in purity and power, except by means of substantial preaching.

Dr. P. F. Bresee epitomized good preaching in a few words when he said that good preaching is so simple that children can understand it, and so spiritual that old people will appreciate it, and in between the children and old people everybody will find his share.

2. The Community, as Distinguished from the Church, Demands Substantial Preaching

It has been said that our day is a difficult one for preachers because of the competition. The community is full of people who are willing to address their fellows publicly on all sorts of subjects and on a wide variety of occasions, so that the preacher no longer has a monopoly on the occasions which call for public speaking. Likewise, it is said that the preacher was once also the teacher and the doctor in the community, and these activities have been taken over by others, so that the preacher is at a disadvantage in having his field restricted.

Even though we may not follow the motto "Competition is the life of trade" through all its meanderings in the philosophy of economics, we do know that specialization is a good thing for efficiency, and that cooperation is more effective in groups than in the community in general. If one were going to make automobile tires, he would do better in Akron, Ohio, than is some community where such work is not done. If he were going to start a department store or a garage, it would be better for him to go into the section of the city where such institutions are generally found. Even if one is going to start a church, it is often better for him to locate on "Church Street" than to go into a section where there are no churches. Since others have taken over schoolteaching and medicine and other branches of service involving learning in general, the minister is better able to specialize on his own God-given task, and he should be able to do that work better than his predecessors could do it cluttered up, as they necessarily were, with "many things." And as to competition from many speakers, let the preacher rejoice that he has so many helpers, and let him prepare to meet the competition by converting it into cooperation. Let others speak on politics, civic reform, and community uplift; and let the preacher give himself to the best message of all—the message that underlies every worthwhile message—the saving message of Christ. And let the preacher preach a better gospel than the others can preach, let him believe a better creed than others believe, let him speak more vitally than the others can speak, and he can be assured of a hearing. The preacher cannot, to be sure, expect to gain a hearing by the grace of his ordination or by the influence of his degrees—the world is not impressed by these things. He must win his hearing on the merits of what he says and the way he says it. But the true prophet of God who is ready and willing to put his best and his all into his task will ask for no better odds than that.

The rights of the community, as well as the rights of the church, deserve consideration. We all have heard how Mary, Queen of Scots, said she feared the prayers of John Knox more than the armies of England. But it was the fearless preaching of Knox that made his prayers a power with the worldly queen. The Scriptures express pity for a people when their king is a child; and in the language of our present thought, that means that the community is in peril when its preachers are weak. John Wesley and the early Methodists are credited with saving England from revolution like that which drenched France with blood. And it was by their awakening of the public conscience, along with the transformation of a comparatively few from sin to holiness, that enabled the British to turn the round corner instead of the square one, as the French did, if they did really turn the corner at all.

Thoughtful men, even though they be wicked and worldly, appreciate virile preaching. Only unregenerated church members and soft hypocrites call for an emasculated gospel and a meaningless message. Even though men may not themselves believe what the preacher says, they feel better if they can realize that the preacher believes it, and believes it with all his heart. Preachers who have been popular with the world have been preachers of the substantial sort. And speaking of the demand as a need, the community certainly demands substantial preaching nowadays. Graft in politics, dishonesty in business, and lasciviousness in social relations all find their going difficult in a land where fearless prophets lift up their voices like trumpets to show the house of David and the people of Israel their sins. That some will not hear, that many will reject and persecute, and that many will not acknowledge the Source of their benefits should not deter the prophet of God; for he does not ask praise, even though he strives to be praiseworthy.

3. The Preacher's Own Soul Demands Substantial Preaching

In fulfilling his duty to God and to his neighbor, one cannot fail to take care of his own soul. And, reversed, if one is true to himself, he cannot be false to any man. Is the preacher a watchman upon the wall? Then, if he is to live with his own conscience, he must lift up his voice like a trumpet when he sees danger approach. Is the preacher a shepherd? Then he must seek the lost with a concern that is all-consuming. Is he a prophet of the gospel age? Then he must shout aloud his tidings of great joy. Is he conscious of his charge to keep? Then he must not shun to make known to men all the counsel of God in the most effective manner it is given him to know it.

I have called it "substantial preaching" in this section, for I have in mind a combination of substance and force that defies definition. The kind of preaching I have in mind is the kind you wish you could do when you cannot do it. Its receipt calls for content and for consecrated personality. Of these factors we shall speak in more detail later. But at the moment we must emphasize that the type of preaching demanded makes heavy draft upon those who would answer to it. It demands religious experience that is as clear and definite as a sunbeam. It demands conviction such as sustained the martyrs while the fagots were being kindled at their feet. It demands patience in preparation like that which Moses had during his days in the Arabian Desert; for it requires the mastering of the doctrines upon which the teaching side of our holy religion is based, and the exercise of the logic and philosophy necessary to enable one to make deep thoughts intelligible. It demands right attitudes toward God, the Church, and the world of mankind. It demands an emptying of selfishness, and an infilling of love that makes one glad to become a follower of the foot-washing Saviour, who sought to minister, not to be ministered unto, and who laid down His life for those He came to serve.

Charles Silvester Horne, in *The Romance of Preaching*, says:

> The appearance of a true preacher is the greatest gift that any nation can have. By his presence, and his spirit, he multiplies the fighting forces for righteousness indefinitely. John Knox's voice was as the sound of a trumpet. When Luther rode to Worms, every timid believer in the Reformation plucked up heart to speak and act more boldly. When Cromwell arrived on Marston Moor, the historian tells us that a great shout went up in the Puritan camp which was the presage of victory.

Later, speaking of the preacher's personal reactions, Horne says:

> There is no tragedy in all the world like the disillusioned minister. He has to keep on preaching. His congregation is often weary; but no one is so heavy of heart as he is.

In summing up, Mr. Horne presents Moses as "the first of the prophets;" the preachers of the Apostolic Age as the leaders of a triumphant movement that remade the world; Athanasius and Chrysostom he calls "the Royalty of the Pulpit;" Savonarola, Calvin, and Knox are "the Rulers of Peoples;" John Robinson and the Pilgrim Fathers are "the Founders of Freedom;" while Wesley and Whitefield represent "the Passion of Evangelism." And in a final word, this preacher whose life span was only 49 years, 25 of which he spent in the active Christian ministry, and when within three days of his own death (although he knew it not) said:

> I have recalled to you, in the course of these lectures, some of the memorable words and deeds of those whose names are inscribed in letters of gold on the roll of the Church's leaders and prophets. It would have been a great thing no doubt to have run with Timothy on some errand for St. Paul. It would have been a great thing to have dared everything for Christ when Nero was on the throne. It would have been a great thing to have confronted emperors with Athanasius, to have died for freedom with Savonarola, to have crossed the Atlantic with Brewster and Bradford, to have walked the world to new spiritual life with Whitefield and Wesley. But let no man say that our age is inferior in opportunity to

any that has gone before. The one demand is the consecrated spirit, and the forward mind.

It will belong to your ministry to conserve for men and women of today the eternal truths in which our fathers lived, but to present those truths as they have passed through the living mind and been shined upon by the broadening light, that is the precious gift of God to our generation.

We may not know the order in which all the things of nature appeared. But we know that there was first a preacher, then a church; and we know that is the order of rank, as well as the order of time. The church of today is what the preachers of yesterday made it, plus the little that the preachers of today have done. The church of tomorrow is prefigured in the preachers of today, and in those who will be the preachers in the near tomorrow. I say this not to our praise, but to emphasize our responsibility. It cannot well be otherwise.

Let us know that while men may choose their civil leaders, and economic overlords may assume their office, ours is a calling in which the eternal God is the sole electorate. This is not an honor that any man can properly take for and of himself. Neither is it an honor that one can properly refuse, if the God of all indicates that he has been chosen. But "a call to service is a call to prepare for service," as well as a call to serve. And none who know the full implications of this calling can ever feel that he has arrived in such a sense that he need no longer apply himself to the best there is, both in preparation and in endeavor to achieve. For only by all available means can anyone become "a good minister of Jesus Christ, nourished up in the words of faith and of good doctrine," to the praise of the glory of Him who hath loved us and washed us in His blood, and made us partakers of the inheritance of the saints in light. To Him be glory both now and forevermore, world without end. Amen.

2

The Substance of Preaching Appraised

All of us have at one time or another read the story of the commonplace things in the lives of the great and wondered why such matters were considered important. George Washington commonly ate corn cakes for breakfast. Many other people also ate corn cakes for breakfast. But the difference was that George Washington did something else besides eating corn cakes for breakfast, and that something else that he did lent value to his ordinary habit.

The greatest human factor in preaching is the preacher himself. A "boy preacher" may occasion a sensation, but he of necessity wants for time to live so that his preaching may become an expression of experience, as well as of theory and observation. A shallow thinker may occasionally say good things, but even good sayings sound better when they come after thinking, rather than before. Preaching implies that the truth of God has passed through a living mind and heart on its way to the hearer's mind and heart. Abstract truth, just truth detached from personality, is not preaching, no matter by what means or under what circumstances it is communicated.

The preacher is, in the true sense, the measure of the sermon. The first step toward becoming a good preacher is to become a good man. The story of a successful preacher of the Apostolic Age is told in the sentence, "He was a good man, full of the Holy Ghost and of faith." There were, of course, many other factors in this soul-winning preacher that served him well. Our surmise is that the was a man of good family connections, that he had good bodily health, that he had a fair education, that he was a man fully saved by the grace of God, and was tactful and talented. But the essential thing was that He was a man fully saved by the grace of God, and filled with and anointed by the Holy Ghost. His qualities were not such as would make him spectacular, but they were such as would make him efficient. Barnabas fell into the category suggested by Phillips Brooks, the class of people who do not so much do miracles, as that they are miracles themselves. One would just expect that a good man, filled with the Holy Ghost and faith, would preach effectively; that people would be impressed by his preaching, as well as by the truth he preached; that they would believe and be saved; and then, as believers, receive comfort and assurance through him.

That indefinable something we call personality is the indispensable factor in preaching. And when it comes to the idea of personality, we are all prone to become fatalists in self-defense. We say, or at least imply, that personality is something that God gives or withholds, and that we are not to blame for not possessing it. But in all such instances we are looking at the varnish, and not at the oak of which the ark is actually constructed. God does indeed give men their personality, but He gives it to them in embryo, as He does the other factors of life. What those about us do, and what circumstances contribute are important, but it is our own application and responses that really tell the story.

Titles like "Pushing to the Front" and psychological ideas about forcing our way in or forcing others out are beside the point for us. Our task is not to find praise but to become praiseworthy. It matters little whether all 10 turn back to give thanks; the important thing is, Do we possess the virtue to cleanse the 10 lepers?

Describing his minister, an old Scotsman said, "When he is in the pulpit, he preaches so well that I wish he would never come down out of it. When he is out of the pulpit, he lives so poorly that I wish he would never go back into the pulpit." But what this story does not tell is that such a preacher is better known both in reputation and by his accomplishments for what he is than for what he says. The preacher is before the sermon to hinder it or to make it effective; and in the process of preparing to preach, building the preacher is more important than building the sermon.

But after the preacher comes the substance of preaching, and it is of this substance that we are to speak in the present section. In the order of thought, the message is father to the sermon, just as the purpose is director of the form. The message is or should be, at least in the preacher's thinking, the heart of the sermon, and the purpose should determine the order in which the sermon should appear.

In one of the conferences connected with Wilbur Chapman's "simultaneous revivals," a pastor complained that he did not have material for revival preaching. But Wilbur Chapman asked that preacher to come to the church where he was to preach that evening, saying, "I plan to preach a sermon which I first preached on Sunday morning as a pastoral sermon. I plan to give the same material tonight; but since it is my purpose to close with an invitation to people to make instant decision for Christ, I shall let this purpose dictate the order; and the sermon which I once used to encourage Christian people, I will use tonight to induce unsaved people to seek and find Christ."

The most common weakness in preaching is its want of "soul." I use this word *soul* in an accommodated sense, but with a meaning that I think is readily understood. I cannot use the term *spirit* without running the risk of having it thought that I speak of enthusiasm or even of demonstration. *Soul,* in the sense I use the term here, is something more fundamental than zeal or demonstration or emphasis or force. It involves timeliness, truth, application, and spiritual unction. This soul in preaching is the source and foundation of preparation. And this preparation is a preparation of the preacher rather than a preparation of material, and its fruitage is the message, not the sermon.

It has been said that great preaching requires three things: (1) a great preacher, (2) a great theme, (3) a great occasion. But under such a definition there can be very little great preaching; so we had better seek a different approach and say that it is better to preach well consistently than to balance off a little great preaching with an overabundance of mediocre preaching or worse. At the railway station in a city where there was a well-known preacher, I overheard two traveling men talking of this preacher and his church. They had themselves attended that church the previous Sunday, and one of them remarked, "You can always count on hearing a good sermon when you go to that church." And I happened to know that that church was usually well attended.

The substance or subject matter of preaching should be:

1. The Bible

Andrew Blackwood says he was inspired to write his book on *Preaching from the Bible* by the question of the chairman of a committee in quest of a pastor. Said that layman, "Where can we find a minister who knows how to preach from the Bible? Our people loved our minister but soon grew weary of his sermons. Every year, after the first few weeks in the fall, he seemed to be all preached out."

H. E. Armacost remarks on the absurdity of the average list of Sunday sermon subjects that appear in the Saturday press, and thinks it little wonder that many preachers lament, "We have piped unto you, and ye have not danced; we have mourned unto you, and ye have not lamented." But underneath these shallow, if not absurd, topics is a want of conviction on the part of preachers; and their platitudinous sermons, administered in homeopathic doses, are indexes to and confessions of a want of authority and a sense of confusion.

Martin Luther, John Wesley, and others have been listed as men of one Book. But this does not mean they did not read other books besides the Bible. It means simply that the Bible was their one authoritative Book, and that other books served to illustrate and enforce, but not to enlighten in the fundamental sense. Their attitude was, and ours should be, "To the law and to the testimony, and if they speak not according to these, it is because there is no light in them."

The Bible needs no particular defense at our hands. It will defend itself if we but preach it. Not much is gained by pulpit and public textual criticism. The preacher does well to examine the Hebrew and the Greek in the privacy of his study, and he may find help in the modern versions and translations.

The preacher must know his Bible. He must know its primary teachings. He should know all the Bible says on all the important subjects of doctrine and ethics. A literary man once asked Ruskin if he had a concordance; Ruskin replied, "I am ashamed to admit that I have." If a literary man could demand of himself an acquaintance with the Book that made a concordance unnecessary, how much more should the man whose chief stock-in-trade is that Book?

It is not within our scope to enlarge upon such questions as the relative value of expository preaching and other approaches to the task of presenting the teachings of the Bible and bringing them to bear upon the lives and consciences of men. Those are matters which call for study and application, and which must be approached from the personal perspective. Strict expository preaching is possible to some and is useful to a few. But every individual will be wise to seek an adaptation that suits his ability and possibilities.

Our challenge here is a wide and general one. It is: Make the Bible known. Make the people hear what the Bible says. Preach the Bible. Explain it whenever you can and explain it interestingly. But do not "explain it away." And do not make explanations that are more difficult than the matter to be explained. Know your Bible and make your hearers know it. Know it in accurate quotation. Know it in its general scope. Know what it says and all it says on every important theme. Know its words. Know its spirit. Know its purpose. Know the Book and make it your principal stock-in-trade, and make others know it, too.

2. Christian Doctrine

There is a current fad which seeks to demote Christian doctrine. But doctrine is just the logical putting of truth, and surely no one will argue that illogical putting is superior to logical. Take a statement made in a recent gathering of returned veterans where request was made to know what the returning veterans desire in religion; the statement was that these veterans do not want doctrine, they just want Christ.

But if Christ is presented, how shall He be presented? Shall we present Him as divine or human? Shall we present Him as virgin born or naturally conceived? Shall we acclaim Him as the Miracle Worker that Matthew, Mark, Luke, and John present? Shall we go on to the Cross and talk of His blood which cleanses from all sin? Shall we follow to the empty tomb and the first Easter morning? Shall we watch Him ascend into heaven from the top of Olivet? Shall we go at His command to the Upper Room for the baptism with the Spirit? Shall we open our hearts to His spiritual in-incoming and indwelling? Shall we talk of the blessed hope of His second coming? Shall we talk of all these things logically? If we do, well, this is doctrine. If we don't, then we are deteriorating in practice and are erring fundamentally by claiming that chaos is superior to order.

The preacher does well not to claim to know what has not been clearly revealed. He does well to keep his essential creed as short as he may. But he is worthless unless he believes something, and he is strong in proportion to how strongly he believes that which is essential. This statement is especially applicable to the positive theses of the faith. It is the fault of the weak that his philosophy is negative. The agnostic takes the easy way in that he leaves his mind suspended. No one can successfully attack the agnostic's position, for he holds no position; and the best you can do is to strike where he was, for you cannot strike where he is now. But all negative philosophy has this strength—and this uselessness.

The man of sound logic never says, "I do not believe." He says, "I believe," and goes on to state his conclusion as regards the matter. I say not, "I do not believe that the organized, material universe came into being by natural, evolutionary processes." I proclaim my positive faith by saying, "I believe that in the beginning God created the heaven and the earth." It is true that my positive assertion opens the way for some to boldly attack me; but, in the meantime, I believe what I believe and do not have to have the opposition of doubters to bolster me up.

Let us take the short creed found in the *Manual* of the Church of the Nazarene, under

"The Reception of Church Members." The statement is introduced by the wise observation that "the doctrines upon which the church rests as essential to Christian experience are brief." Then comes the compact list:

> We believe in God the Father, Son, and Holy Ghost, we especially emphasize the deity of Jesus Christ and the personality of the Holy Spirit; that man is born in sin; that he needs the work of the Holy Spirit in regeneration; that, after the work of regeneration, there is the further work of heart-cleansing, or entire sanctification, which is effected by the Holy Ghost. And to each of these works of grace the Holy Spirit gives witness. We believe in eternal destiny, with its rewards and punishments.

This is what we believe. It is what we believe in epitome. In working out such a creed, all the phases and implications of systematic and biblical theology are embraced. But in working out to the circumference of so imposing a system, there is room for much care, and call for much clarity. Our insistence is not on either a wide or a long creed, but on one of such essential truth that one can afford to live and die for its defense.

It is not accidental that the very term *preach* has come to indicate dogmatism. One does not preach who speaks in apology. He preaches only when he speaks with authority. Therefore a man cannot preach that which he does not believe, or that which he believes but uncertainly. This is why testimony is the strongest form of preaching, for in testimony there is little room for the miscarriage of logic—one is just telling what he has seen and heard and felt; and within this sphere he speaks with authority.

In the interpretation of experience there may be uncertainty; but in the facts of the experience itself, there is no ground for doubt. Peter knew he saw a vision on the housetop, a vision of the sheet let down from heaven with many kinds of birds and beasts on it. But he was not sure what the vision was meant to signify until he listened to the committee from the house of Cornelius, come to invite him to preach the gospel to the Gentiles. Then at once he concluded, "God hath shown me that I should not call any man common or unclean."

A unique orator said, "You cannot catch souls with question marks." And the maxim is worthy of a wider application. You cannot really give anyone assurance in matters in which you are not sure yourself. But I would not knowingly mix experiential and theoretical assurance; and since it is of doctrine and not experience that we are speaking, I mingle the exhortation not to be dogmatic in things that may be doubted, with the challenge that you know some things, be they ever so few in number; and that you know them so well that you preach them as truths—understood or not understood. Even the fact that you may not be able to prove your theses to the other man's satisfaction and must, on that account, excuse his want of full agreement, you must be fully persuaded in your own mind. Instead of compromising with those who are yet unconvinced, it is your task to convince them and find agreement on the higher plane of truth rather than on the low plane of uncertainty.

Speaking of "The Essentials of a Sermon," in the book called *Preaching,* G. Campbell Morgan says the essentials of a sermon are "truth, clarity, and passion." In enlarging upon the idea of truth, Dr. Morgan says that truth is the final fact about Jesus; and that any sermon that fails to have some interpretation of holy truth is a failure. On the point of clarity, he quotes Martin Luther as saying, "'A preacher ought so to preach, that when the sermon is ended, the congregation shall disperse saying, "The preacher said this."'" We preach in order that people may apprehend, and when we fail in that, we fail.

Dr. Morgan suggests that if we had in mind to use a certain word and then found out that 20 people in the congregation do not know what the word means, we should strike it out; and he thinks we should be so faithful to this as it relates to the main idea that even our illustrations should be chosen with it in mind. We should make as sure as we can that people will not be drawn away from the main theme in their following of the illustration. On the point of passion, Dr. Morgan suggests that if the preacher can preach without passion, then what he is preaching is not really truth to him.

Just as it is the first obligation of the preacher to make sure that he understands the meaning of his text, and that he is faithful to the teachings of the text, the context, and the whole general trend of the Bible, so, in the second place, he should measure his thesis always by the touchstone of sound doctrine. It is a temptation to many to be eclectic; that is, to believe and preach tenets that are inconsistent with one another. Take a subject like millenarianism, for example. The truth must lie, fundamentally, between postmillenarianism and premillenarianism. It is much easier to get in between these and hold something like panmillenarianism, taking what suits from either of the two and making a composite which is sentimentally more agreeable. But the bug that is composed of the body of one bug, the wings of another, and the legs of another, must in the end be but a humbug.

Or take historic Calvinism and Arminianism: These two systems of thought at their base are divided on five principal and closely related theses: (1) on the question of whether or not election is conditional, (2) on the question of whether or not grace is resistible, (3) on the question of whether or not the will of man is bound, (4) on the question of whether or not the atonement is limited, (5) on the question of whether final perseverance is conditional or not. Now the truth must lie with one or the other of the alternates. The consistent Calvinist believes in unconditional election, irresistible grace, a bound will, a limited atonement, and final, unconditional perseverance. The consistent Arminian believes in conditional election, resistible grace, a free will, an unlimited atonement, and in final, conditional perseverance.

And each of these must believe in all five theses of his system to be consistent in any of them. That is, belief in any of these theses involves the system of which it is a tenet. But it is easier to believe in conditional election, resistible grace, a free will, an unlimited atonement; and then jump over, after all these have been posited, and claim unconditional final perseverance for the subjects of regenerating grace. The premises are Arminian, the conclusion Calvinistic. This hodgepodge comes out in the modern composite which makes a maxim of "eternal security."

No honest man can be an eclectic unless he be essentially illogical by nature. It is like running your train down a certain track and then when a grade or fill or bridge is encountered, jump right over onto some parallel track without going to the trouble to provide for a rational and real transference. Passing thinkers have smiled at the determination of some to be logical, even if wrong; but that is a necessity with an honest thinker; for to him to be illogical is to tell a lie.

There is, as we know, a modern nondoctrinal fallacy. The idea being that you can preach Christ without preaching any doctrines concerning Him, that you can preach salvation without doctrinal interpretation, and that you can enjoin Christian duty without making a thesis of ethics. But a plea for such is on a par with the plea for a method of making a living without work. In fact, there is justification for Dr. W. J. Dawson's quaint saying to the effect that "half the bad theology in the world is due to suppressed perspiration." Lazy preachers substitute words for thought, and lazy people would rather hear soft words than be faced with the call for hard thinking. But we see the apostolic example represented by the charge the court filed against those early preachers, saying, "You have filled Jerusalem with your doctrines."

It might be supposed that there would be a third division in this section. We have presented the Bible and Christian doctrine as being involved in the substance of preaching, and it might be supposed that we would add "Christian life." But Christian life comes more directly within the scope of application than of substance. Its field is covered when the truths of the Bible and of Christian doctrine are brought to bear upon the character and conduct of men. The ethics of Christianity are involved in the doctrines of Christianity, for the basis of Christian conduct is not a list of rules of thumb, but an application of high and inclusive principles.

Take the Sabbath question as an example. The law of the Christian Sabbath is that it is a day set apart for rest and worship, that rest and worship are obligatory, though works of mercy and of necessity may be done on the day. That sounds simple, and it is simple until one begins to apply the principle to detailed practice; and especially when he begins to try to think for others than himself. The farmer is sure that feeding his stock, milking his cows, and taking care of his poultry are works of necessity, if not also works of mercy. But in complicated civilized communities, what about operating the buses, keeping the electric plants going, and standing by certain continuous operations, like keeping the fires going in factories, ships, and shops?

Or take the dress question. Our *Manual* says: "Our people are to dress with the Christian simplicity and modesty that becometh holiness." That is simple and fundamental. But when you come to apply it, there are as many ideas as there are people, and some people are not consistent even in their own judgment of the meaning of the principle.

Or take the liquor question. The basis of objection to liquor from any approach is that alcohol is injurious to the human body when used as a beverage. On this principle there is agreement. But in the implications of the whole subject, especially as related to the control or destruction of the liquor traffic, there is want of uniformity. Some vehemently hold that unless one votes the Prohibition party ticket, he is party to the liquor traffic. Others say that more than liquor is involved in the responsibility of the franchise, and they vote tickets other than the Prohibition party ticket and still claim they are for the obliteration of the liquor traffic.

Even economics becomes a moral issue with many. I have heard a well-known preacher present Christianity as an economic system standing with Communism on one side and

Fascism on the other, and begging to be taken in lieu of one of the others.

Divorce—all agree on the principle that divorce is an evil that threatens the home and the nation; but there are many suggestions as to how to manage the evil, and all claim that their method of handling it is the way of morality and righteousness or else the way of mercy and salvation.

Take the duties of church membership. All agree that "the privileges and blessings which we have in association together in the Church of Jesus Christ are very sacred and precious." And that "there is in it such hallowed fellowship as cannot otherwise be known." And none question that in the membership of the Church "there is cooperation in service, accomplishing that which cannot otherwise be done." But when there is an attempt to reduce this to inflexible rules of thumb, it is found necessary to allow for a certain amount of variation of interpretation. In our church, it can be truthfully said, I think, that most of our people are tithers. Still we have never thought it wise to make the practice of tithing a condition of membership. And among those who are tithers, there is still the question of "storehouse tithing" to be met. We have never deemed it wise to try to think for all our people on the subject of the mode of baptism.

In fact, our church has for the most part confined its requirements both in doctrine and in practice to principles; and time serves, more and more, I think, to indicate the wisdom of this course. But this is the hard way. The easy way would be to make rules of thumb, to require uniformity, to prescribe a uniform to be worn by our women and our men respectively, to define our position and required practice on the use of the civil franchise, to set hard and fast definitions, and to demand agreement therewith. But, in the end, no one can be righteous accidently, nor can holiness be inculcated by force. One might conform outwardly and be vicious inwardly.

From the preacher's perspective, the demand is for clear thinking, clean living, clear judgment, sound conviction, and everlasting application to the task of instruction. Our people must know the truth as it applies to Christian ethics and life, and they must follow in the paths of righteousness and true holiness of their own free will and choice. They must be intelligent as well as consistent Christians. They must do right, knowing it is right, and they must shun the wrong, being convinced that it is wrong. Thus there is set before our preachers a big and never ending task.

The preacher is to be "a man under authority," but it is to be the authority of truth, not the authority of force. There are children in our churches, but all our people are not children; and while the children may someday become adults, the adults will never again become children, unless indeed tragic calamity befall them. We cannot therefore count much on using that authority that comes through force, but must rely on that authority that comes simply from being right and being wise. Ours is the authority of leadership and not the authority of rulership. We must therefore look well to our theses for truth and sobriety.

We must be patient as teachers, and yet not give away the ideal in exchange for the easy real. It is but a weak preacher who says, "I will do and say just what others are doing and saying." Rather he must do and say what in his conception is true and right, regardless of the delinquencies of others. If, in such a process, he becomes *persona non grata* with his brethren, then he must accept his nonacceptability as the price of his fidelity; he must neither contend nor complain. That is the spirit of the martyrs, and it is the spirit of every good man of true conviction. It is only by such men that the gospel of Jesus Christ can be preached, and Christian standards lifted and sustained.

In matters that pertain to their present good and their eternal salvation, people have a right to ask for everything that a preacher can do in the way of personal preparation, Bible knowledge, sound doctrine, and sane application. In the course of human life on earth, marriage and death are, perhaps, the two most serious matters, having to do with happiness on earth and with destiny in the world to come. These subjects are not joking matters, and jokes about them are practically all coarse, uncalled for, and detrimental. Yet it is the habit of men to joke about things they fear. The wise person fears an unhappy union in marriage, and an untimely death or a death for which he is unprepared. But instead of making these subjects matter for prayer and earnest thought, it is easier to joke about them and to make as though they are light matters after all. Some people may do this same thing about God and religion. But religion is the third thing concerning which joking is altogether out of place.

Religion is indeed like a strong medicine which the doctor gives as a last resort, knowing that it will either kill or cure—either kill the patient or cure him of his disease. If religion is all some claim it is, then it is worth every sacrifice and seeming sacrifice that its possession involves. But if it is not that, then it is of small consequence and should be disregarded by intelligent people. Can one be truly intelligent and yet be a Christian? Some people do not seem to think so, and hence they make religion a light and airy thing, or else assign it an alternate place, like the scribes and Pharisees attempted to do with John's baptism. But John, you know, would permit no such mixture of motives. Either these impenitents whom he likened to serpents and vipers should come hanging their hopes on God through the medium of the conditions the wilderness preacher set forth, or they could turn back to such consolation as they might be able to find in the shell-like forms of a dead faith.

Preachers must know the truth, they must preach the truth; and they must preach it soberly, substantially, and passionately. The actors on the stage draw their crowds by presenting fiction as though it were truth; but preachers cannot reverse this order with telling effect. Preachers must preach the truth as it is indeed—the truth. There are times, I know, when the passing popularity of shallow entertainers and ear-tickling orators bring a sense of depression to the dispenser of truth "as it is in Christ Jesus." It is annoying to see even "faithful members" turning to a nondoctrinal ministry in some tabernacle or taking up with some shadowy fad or wistful fancy in religion. But ours is a character rather than a reputation calling. Meteors light up the sky more brightly than the fixed stars, but they pass quickly into the discard and leave the night to the constant stars. No man who cannot discern between appearance and reality, and who does not value character above reputation, can qualify as a substantial preacher of the everlasting gospel.

To be entirely consistent with the ideal herein presented, the true preacher of the true faith must avoid handling the Word of God deceitfully or lightly by positing interpretations that are either false or doubtful. This statement, of course, has its limitations, else no man could venture to preach. But within the limits that we all know exist as regarding such matters, the preacher must be fully persuaded in his own mind. He cannot take a text that to him manifestly means one thing (like the fire of Isaiah 33 which clearly refers to God) and preach something else (like a sermon on hell) from it as a basis. He cannot take a theme like the second coming of Christ and make it the occasion for a lot of speculation and spectacular guesses by means of which he is likely to gain a reputation as "an expert." He cannot take a parable that clearly emphasizes one phase of truth and "throw it down on its all-fours" and cause his hearers to get lost in the maze.

He cannot take a scripture passage that evidently has a local setting and stretch it to cover some hobby of his own. He cannot indulge in half-baked ideas about doctrine, ethics, life, and conduct by means of which he definitely contributes to the removal of the central principle from its position and makes an apparent passing matter take the place of an eternal verity.

As a final exhortation, and using the language of the military, we suggest that we keep our battle lines short, look well to the reserves, and keep in mind that winning the war is more important than winning a given battle. This means, in clerical language, confine your creed to the essentials—do not spread your orthodoxy over too much scope. It means, believe the essentials, believe them with all your heart, and preach them without regard to either the fear or the favor of men. Do not claim to know everything about anything or anything about everything; but do be an authority on the way to God, and be a prophet. Within this scope yield to nobody.

Do not be content with current preaching material only. Insist on possessing such abundance that always you can "preach out of the overflow" and give only the cream of your thought. Keep in mind that it is better to win a man to Christ by patience and persistence than to either drive him away or drive him in as a puppet. Remember that "the church is not a museum for the exhibition of eminent saints," as Beecher once said, "but a workshop for the production of useful Christians." The Church is not built by attachments, as rocks are believed to be, but by the inward processes of absorption and enlargment, like trees.

Fiction is sometimes stranger than truth, and some people are devotees of the new and the spectacular. But in the long run, fiction loses out in the race with truth; and as Christians and Christian preachers, the long run is the run we are on. Henry Clay is praised for preferring to be right instead of preferring to be president, and we likewise do well to elect to be dispensers of that truth that will never pass away instead of choosing to be popular for a day or a week or a year or even a lifetime with those who are willing to sacrifice the interests of eternity upon the altars of time. "Heaven and earth shall pass away, but my words shall not pass away" (Matt. 24:35).

3

The Force of Preaching Estimated

Those who listened to Jesus were impressed with what He said, but they were also impressed by the way He said it, "for he taught them as one having authority," and not in that method of indirection which many of the times were accustomed to use. His "but I say unto you" was in exact contrast to the appeal to contemporaneous authorities and to notable men of the past, which was the way the scribes sought to sustain their interpretations of law and of life.

Complaints that preachers are "too dogmatic" arise from one or two faults, so far as the preachers are concerned: (1) Either the preacher does not really know, and seeks to cover his ignorance by a positive attitude; or (2) what he knows is of secondary importance and therefore invites debate. If we attempt to approach the matter from the perspective of the objectors, it may be that the objections to the preacher's positive attitude are based upon a faulty life, an insecure testimony, or a poorly supported creed.

The positive preacher must confine his dogmatism to his own field, and that field is religion—more restrictedly, revealed religion, Bible religion. It is well that the preacher know something of history, philosophy, literature, science, and art; but the gods of these realms are so exacting that one cannot worship at more than one of these altars, and he must worship there continuously to be worthy of a place among the honorables. The preacher, therefore, is, and should acknowledge himself to be, before anyone has time to accuse him, a novice and an amateur in every branch and every calling outside his own. The old saw about "jack of all trades and master of none" is increasingly applicable as knowledge increases from day to day. The know-it-all preacher is a menace to his own trade as well as a thorn in the side of honest people of all trades.

Even within the legitimate scope of his own field, the preacher must be modest. The scope of theological thought is too wide for one mind to cover it all. The specialized forms of ministerial activity are too many and too varied for one preacher to be good in all of them—if for no other reason than want of opportunity. Much sport has been made of the man who criticizes those who are doing a task better than he can do it himself; and, of course, those who love criticism have their answers. Nevertheless, even within the legitimate scope of the ministry as a whole, and within the limits of each man's specialized work, it is good advice that "every man should abide in the calling wherein he is called," and not be too free with his criticisms of fellow ministers or too liberal in his suggestions as to how he would do it if he were given a chance. Running for office is not a very popular thing in the Christian ministry, and giving people suggestions before they ask for them is a gratuitous and sometimes unappreciated service.

Nevertheless, the preacher who makes a success of preaching must be certain. He must be certain of his own acceptance with God and his integrity before men. He is an ambassador, and his office requires him to be in good grace both with Him who has sent him and with those to whom he is sent. This demands of him that he know the message of God and the language and habits of men. When an angel spoke to Jesus on the streets of Jerusalem, Jesus knew what the angel said; but many bystanders, not knowing the language of angels, said, simply, "It thundered." In that case it was not essential that bystanders hear understandingly, and thunder was impressive enough for the purpose intended. But thundering is not preaching, for while thunder may say something to those who know the language of the elements, it does not say anything intelligible to men of the common sort.

When preachers say great things in high-sounding words and phrases, they may thunder, but they do not preach, for they use not the language of men. To the average listener they are like the bishop in India, who, using a native interpreter, began by saying, "I am going to preach on faith, and I shall begin by saying that faith is both abstract and concrete." The native interpreter had no idea of what *abstract* and *concrete* meant, so he said solemnly to the waiting audience, "The bishop is going to preach on faith. He has not said anything about it yet, and just as soon as he does say something, I will tell you what it is."

We all expect that the foreign missionary will learn the language of the people to whom he goes, but those who have tried say it is just as important to learn the people as it is to learn their language. Those who would simplify the task of the foreign missionary by praying that he might receive the gift of language, instead of having to acquire the language by long, continued study, would need to include in the prayer a request for a gift of both knowledge and wisdom; for it has often proved a godsend that the new missionary cannot speak the language of the people until he has had time to learn the people also. This same principle holds when the language is the mother tongue of the preacher, for it is while he is wrestling with his instrument of expression that he gains both something to express and a knowledge of the people to whom it is to be expressed. God's Book of revelation and His book of nature, for the work of the preacher, are followed closely with the book of human nature.

In speaking, then, of "The Force of Preaching" by way of giving an estimate of it, we porpose to consider four essentials: (1) The clarity and timeliness of the message; (2) the adequacy and expressiveness of the language employed; (3) the ability and adaptability of the preacher as an instrument; and (4) the presence of spiritual unction.

Approaching these factors in this order, we have:

1. The Clarity and Timeliness of the Message

We do not presume to suggest that God ever gives a veiled message to His servants. It is in the reception of the revelation that blurring occurs. As preaching time approaches, the preacher who is sincere in his desire to do good is bound to ask, "What shall I preach?" He knows he cannot hold the audience while he gives them the content of the whole divine revelation. His opportunity is limited by both his own ability and the capacity of those who will hear him, and his question as to what he shall preach has reference to both content and timeliness.

Peter asks that his brethren "be established in the present truth," and that phrase "present truth" is suggestive of timeliness. It is true that God sent a flood of water upon the earth, and a message on that subject was quite timely during the period while Noah was building the ark. But if one preaches on the flood now, he must treat the flood as a fact of history and draw from it lessons which apply to our times; otherwise he is preaching content without timeliness. Nor is this a farfetched instance. Nothing is clearer in the teaching of the New Testament than the fact that the whole revelation of the plan for Jesus to come back to the world the second time (not the fact of His second coming, but the purpose of the revelation of this plan for His coming) was that His disciples might be ready for that coming. And yet many "specialists on prophecy" disregard the crux of the matter, which is that one must be sanctified wholly and robed in Christ's imparted righteousness to be really ready when He appears.

Much of the sport that has been made of the methods of old-time revivalists and camp meeting preachers has been made by those who would substitute a blurred and undefined message for the definite call "to flee the wrath to come" which those early prophets sounded forth. In introducing a sermon on "What Must I Do to Be Saved?" Sam Jones said he would not include anything in his sermon that a man could not do if he were dying. And by these words, the soundness and urgency of his message were emphasized.

There is the story of a preacher who, somewhat knowingly and somewhat imperceptibly, departed from his former evangelistic emphasis, characterized by the call to immediate repentance and faith for salvation, and had substituted in its place a sort of "salvation by character," "nobody-really-lost, nobody-really-saved" theory. All went well until he was urgently called to the deathbed of a sinful woman who earnestly asked him to "help her get in" before death should close the door. Here was a challenge that the preacher's new theories could not meet; but the preacher was too honest and too Christian to forsake the woman who had asked what seemed reasonable of a Christian minister. So the preacher set in for a prayer that lasted the rest of the night. Just as the first rays of the sun appeared through the cracks of the attic hovel of the wretched woman, the light broke in on both the woman and the preacher. The woman went on very soon to the Lord of Light in glory, and the preacher went back to preach the gospel of salvation with urgency—he was as truly converted as she was.

Truth is, of course, the indispensable ingredient of forceful preaching; but in addition to weight, this truth must be presented in concentrated form. A hammer may weigh 50 pounds, but if it is put together as loosely as a bale of hay, it may not be useful in driving a carpet tack into soft pine wood; but even though the hammer may weigh but a few ounces, if it is of compact, blue steel, it will be useful to drive a 20-penny nail into hard oak. The great preachers of the past have all been orthodox on the whole body of Christian truth, but they have, usually unconsciously, been apostles of some one tenet of doctrine about which the whole galaxy of Christian doctrines are held together like the hub unites the wheel.

With Paul, this central thesis was faith; with James it was conduct; with John it was love; with Jude it was judgment. In later times the thesis with Luther was justification by faith; with Knox it was the sovereignty of God; with Fox it was the witness of the Spirit; with Wesley it was sanctification by faith subsequent to justification; with Finney it was the justice of God; with Moody it was the love of God. And in making the partial revelation clear, these men brought into view all that is necessary to salvation and life for all.

We suggest these men as illustrations, not especially as examples to be imitated. The point is, the forceful preacher must see clearly; and if he cannot see clearly and see widely at the same time, he had better see clearly. The astronomers which tell us most about the stars are not the ones who take a nightly glance at the whole celestial universe. Rather they are the ones who patiently study a given spot so carefully that they discover things that escape the casual observer.

I asked a man, who said he was a professor in a state university, in what field he took his work for his doctor's degree. He said he took it in English. When I asked for closer definition, he said he did his work on the word *such,* and that it required three years to complete the task, including the necessity of learning the Anglo-Saxon language and making a card index covering 10,000 references to the word *such* in English and Anglo-Saxon. Pushed still further, the man admitted that he was an authority on the word *such*, and that he knew more about it than any other man living or dead. It was not a big subject, but it was something to be an authority on it.

Forceful preaching must be based upon clarity, and clarity, in turn, is father to assurance. The forceful preacher must have a message, he must know what that message is, and he must be convinced that his message is in the class of indispensables. "Truth for truth's sake" is a high-sounding maxim, but its adoption does not help in the making of forceful preachers. Even though a thing may be true, if one's feeling about it is "So what?" he can never really preach it.

All this goes back to the basic question: What is true? What is important? There is a sense, of course, in which anything that is true is important, but there is also a sense in which some things that are true are of more importance than other things that are true. For example, it is important that a man should have some sort of transportation if he is to make a journey; but it is more important that he should be going somewhere. Every man came from somewhere, that is true. But it is also true that every man is going somewhere, and this is more important.

On that item of timeliness, one more word deserves to be said. Timeliness is not only a matter relating to the calendar and the clock.

It is also a matter which relates to seasons and temperatures. When pioneers were working at the task of making something of commercial value out of crude rubber, they gave first attention to chemistry and tried vainly to find a mixture that would give the combined results required. It was by accident that the missing factor—temperature—was applied, and vulcanization came into being. The mixture would not work in the cold. Forceful preaching must regard the temperature. The wise preacher likes to have the guidance of the worship service (incorrectly dubbed "the preliminaries"), for by means of this he hopes to get himself and his hearers into tune and time for the preaching. But sometimes the worship service is not of the preacher's direction, and sometines when it is, it yet fails of its purpose. In any case, forceful preaching must be in line with the atmosphere, whether the agreement is brought about by a change in the atmosphere or a change in the preacher and a variation of the message.

Speaking from experience, I have sometimes gone to the pulpit expecting to preach on a judgment theme. But as preaching time approached, I found that my own heart was not mellow, and that there was a danger of a show of vindictiveness in manner or voice, and I had to shift over to a mercy theme. I have planned sometimes to preach a strongly doctrinal sermon; but interference, sometimes of a welcome nature, sometimes of a useless sort, consumed the time, so that it appeared quite wise to turn to an inspiration line where arguments are little needed and where conclusion is the main thing.

Candor compels me to admit that I have not always been wise. Sometimes I have pushed on, determined to be faithful to my subject, no matter how merciless this required me to be to my crowd; and I have found myself "preaching in the wilderness" in a sense that John the Baptist seems never to have done.

When the preacher is seeking answer to his own question, What shall I preach? he should carefully consider these supplementary and secondary questions: Is this I think of preaching really true? Am I sure that it is true? Is it important, admitting that it is true? Is this line of truth timely for this occasion and for the hearers that I expect to be present? If I were going to preach just this one last time to this crowd, could I preach on this subject as a dying man to dying men? If I should find it necessary to pay with my life for preaching this sermon, would it be worth it? Is there any other subject that in my thinking and in the burden of my soul would do "just as well"? Why am I choosing this subject rather than some other?

If some unexpected person should be on hand at the service, would I be embarrassed, or would I be like that old preacher who was warned on the eve of his standing up to preach that Gen. Andrew Jackson was in the audience? The old preacher, it is said, stood up in his place at the right time, and, although visibly moved, he found deliverance by rising to this proclamation that was altogether to the General himself. Said the old preacher, "They tell me Gen. Andrew Jackson is in the audience this morning. Who is Gen. Andrew Jackson? If Gen. Andrew Jackson is a sinner, he will die and go to hell just like any other sinner, except he repent." And from then on the old preacher was free.

2. The Adequacy and Expressiveness of the Language Employed

Educators agree that the reason many students cannot learn is because they cannot read; that is, they cannot read understandingly. They cannot read fast enough to get the grasp of the subject, and there are so many words in the text that do not register meaning that the student gets "just a smattering" of the subject in hand. Limitations like this are present always at the preaching service. And although it may be reasoned that the fault is with the hearers for not giving more attention to lexicography, the preacher must meet the situation as it is and make himself understood. The preacher needs a wide vocabulary that he may repeat without monotony.

Repetition is the most familiar method of emphasis, but if the same thought can be presented with synonymous words of varied sound, the hearers will reap the benefits of hearing often without suffering the monotony of humdrum identity. The preacher should know words big and little. He should use little words from choice, not from necessity. But he should use little words, beginning with words of one syllable, and using longer words only when shorter ones are not available. It may sound more elegant to speak of "an agricultural instrument used for the purpose of excavating earth," but more people will get the idea if the preacher calls it a spade.

However, the preacher cannot be seen to stoop. For just as children early come to resent "baby talk," grown people instinctively dislike one who manifestly "comes down" to them. The preacher must think clearly and speak his thoughts clearly. Big words, as Dr. Godbey, used to explain it, are intended as time and space savers, often being sufficient to replace sentences. But more often, big words are just substitutes for little thoughts or for big thoughts that are yet too shadowy to stand the full sunlight of everyday language.

But understood language still has plenty of room for variety and expressiveness; and the speaker, by gesture, diction, and emphasis, can magnify the impression of a word so that a pound word can be made to weigh a ton. George Whitefield, preaching to the sailors, described a storm at sea, in the plain language the sailors knew. So vivid was the picture that at the point where the mast was swept away and the ship became unmanageable, the sailors, wrapped in the reality of the experience pictured, leaped to their feet en masse and cried, "Take to the lifeboats." It was an easy matter for a preacher like that to apply his vivid story to the ship of life and to exhort his seawise hearers to take their places in the lifeboat of salvation.

The old country woman was agreeably surprised when she was able to understand every word John Wesley said in his sermon, but this must not be taken to mean that Wesley was understood only because his language was simple. For his language was expressive as well as simple; and language that is not expressive is weak, even though it may be simple.

The ideal is for the preacher to be able to read foreign languages and then, without ado, interpret what he has read into the mother tongue. He should be able to read and hear big words understandingly, and then say the thoughts of the wise expressively in the ears of those who would not be able to see the thoughts for the words should they undertake to read for themselves.

Every preacher needs to guard against the tendency to be redundant with favorite words and phrases. One preacher, imitating a great pulpit orator whom he admired, introduced so much of his material with the expression "Methinks I see," an expression the orator had used effectively in describing John in the wilderness, that one night a group of young people were heard to say, "Methinks I shall now go home," and the preacher dropped that expression entirely.

There is an oratorical order, as well as grammatical and rhetorical order. We try to observe this order, according to our purpose, in the preparation of sermons. The preacher must have something interesting and important to say during his first five minutes these days, or it is unlikely that many will be still listening when he comes to where he is truly saying something. And, whatever may have been the habits of the past, the preacher must, as an old Texas farmer would say, "keep right up in the collar" all the time. His material should be ordered in such a manner that he "goes from strength to strength." If there is more than one climax, the last must be higher than the first or the effect will be lost.

There is also an oratorical order in the arrangement of paragraphs, sentences, and even of words. We used to be warned against ending a sentence with a preposition. But we should avoid ending a sentence with any sort of weak word. It is proverbial that it is difficult for the preacher to quit. This fault is not only observable as regards the time allotted to the sermon as a whole, but it is also observable with reference to sentences. Instead of saying his say and quitting on the emphatic word and the dominant tone, many a preacher passes the good place to stop and finally concludes like an old-fashioned clock that has simply "run down."

3. The Ability and Adaptability of the Preacher as an Instrument

The terms *ability* and *adaptability* are more related in sound than in meaning. At least, if one has supposed the two to be identical, he has erred. Ability is like knowledge; adaptability is like wisdom. Ability is force, while adaptability is force harnessed to a worthwhile task. Ability is potential character; adaptability is character developed and in action. Ability is static; adaptability is fluid and in motion. Ability is capital in the pocket; adaptability is capital invested and drawing interest. Ability always increases very slowly; adaptability may increase at a rapid pace. These statements are all partial, and in a sense metaphorical—it is not within my power to be either complete or literal with relation to these tremendous factors.

If we were appraising preachers, we would say that the man of ability may preach acceptably, but we would say that the man of adaptability will preach acceptably. The thought is that the man of ability has what it takes, the man of adaptability makes use of what it takes to preach acceptably.

All of you have access to dictionaries and encyclopedias, so I shall not weary you with definitions. Enough that we shall take it that *ability* is the term by which our natural and acquired powers, considered in static form, are described. One form of ability is physical health. This, in a measure, a man inherits from his parents, but it is within his power to increase and preserve the heritage. Power to apprehend and to reason are forms of ability. These, too, may be increased by the possessor. Spiritual forces such as are bestowed by the Holy Spirit are also capable of enlargement, on conditions that the possessor can meet. One increases his physical heritage by the practice of correct hygiene. He increases his intellectual capacity by study and application. He increases his spiritual abilities by prayer and faith and obedience.

Adaptability is a dependent quality, and one who would increase it must go down to the principles that underlie it. He must by grace become unselfish. He must by tact learn not to argue about trifles, and to agree with others in minor matters every time this is possible. He must teach himself to enjoy yielding to others when no principle is involved, and he must practice keeping his lines short that he may spend his time and efforts affecting men in matters that are essential.

But in a more technical sense, the preacher must give himself to preaching, if he would really be a preacher. It is not enough that he make the ministry his vocation. It is not enough that he "fill the pulpit" every time that is expected of him. To be a preacher, a preacher must practice preaching the very best he can every time he stands before an audience. Only a few favored preachers always have large crowds to wait upon their words. But any preacher can deserve a larger crowd by preaching well to the small one. No one can deny that a good crowd is an inspiration, but the good preacher must train himself to preach well when the night is rainy and the crowd is small.

The preacher that preaches well must be a

preacher all the time—in the pulpit and out of it. While others see people and things in the light of their interests, the preacher must see them in the light of his calling. He must hold fast to the homiletical instinct when he reads, he must keep preaching in mind when he looks, and he must pass all he hears through his own mill in the endeavor to find something that will help him preach.

When the moment for preaching arrives, the adaptable preacher will throw his full weight into the exercise. Head, heart, and hand—the preacher will lay tribute upon them all in his effort to preach with becoming force. The worst feeling anyone can have toward an honest preacher is that he is not doing as well as he is capable of doing, and the worst of all habits on the part of the preacher is the habit of holding back on either material or effort in the hope of a better opportunity. The opportunity is the gift of God, and it is the preacher's duty to make the most of it. No preacher is so good that anything less than his best is ever acceptable.

4. The Presence of Spiritual Unction

Spiritual unction is something we cannot define, but something we very much miss when it is not present. It is that divine thing which resting upon a preacher differentiates gospel preaching from every other form of public discourse.

The idea of unction, of course, harks back to the ancient practice of anointing with oil as a symbol of consecration to an office or order. But even then, the oil was a symbol of the spiritual. The term also has been used in a lower sense to describe mere human emotion or that element in speech that excites emotion in others. But both the symbols and the counterfeit point toward the genuine. There is promised to those that preach the gospel a spirit of wisdom that adversaries will not be able to gainsay, and there is promised also to them a divine touch that gives point and pith to their speech, and gives it power to penetrate not only the intelligences of men, but their consciences as well.

The preparation of the preacher's heart is of no less importance than the preparation of his mind; for while his doctrine is the channel, the Holy Spirit is the power. A teacher of elocution went to hear Bishop Matthew Simpson, telling a friend that his purpose was to make a study of the bishop's elocution. At the climax of his sermon, when he was telling how God in pardoning mercy takes away the burden of sin, the preacher assumed a stooped posture as he approached his high point. At the critical moment, the preacher suddenly lifted his shoulders and stood bold upright, indicating that a load had been lifted from his back. When this gesture came, the audience arose to its feet as though it were but one man. Later the friend asked the elocution teacher what he thought of the bishop's elocution. The man who had gone to think of art replied, "Elocution! Bishop

Simpson does not need elocution, he has the Holy Ghost."

John D. Fulsom, in *The Holy Spirit Our Helper*, says:

> At whatever cost, the minister must appear before his people as a man sent from God, and speak as moved by the Holy Spirit. No social popularity, no intellectual gifts, however much admired, no administrative success, no pastoral diligence will suffice for him. If he stand not before his people with a seer's vision, a prophet's boldness, and with an unction of the Holy Spirit, he falls below his high calling. "The Holy Spirit," says Spurgeon, "must rest upon your preachers. Let them have all the learning of the wisest men, and all the eloquence of such men as Demosthenes and Cicero, still the word cannot be blessed to you, unless, first of all, the Spirit of God hath guided the minister's mind in the selection of his subject and in the discussion of it." Of the Holy Spirit's power when resting on the preacher, he says, "Our words are now full of life and flame. They are borne by the breath of the Spirit, and they fall like fire-flakes, and set the souls of men blazing with desire after God. Come on us now, O rushing mighty wind and tongue of fire, for the world hath great need."

Folsom quotes Rev. Nathan Bangs, who was present at the General Conference of the Methodist Episcopal Church in 1808, as follows:

> The Light Street Church was filled to overflowing. I saw the preacher of the morning enter the pulpit, sunburned and dressed in very ordinary clothes, with a red flannel shirt, which showed a large space between his vest and his small clothes. He appeared more like a poor backwoodsman than like a minister of the

gospel. I felt mortified that such a looking man had been appointed to preach on such an imposing occasion. As he advanced in his discourse a mysterious magnetism seemed to emanate from him to all parts of the house. He was absorbed in the interest of his subject. His voice rose gradually till it sounded like a trumpet. At a climacteric passage the effect was overwhelming. It thrilled through the assembly like an electric shock. The house rang with irrepressible responses; many hearers fell prostrate to the floor. An athletic man sitting by my side fell as if shot by a cannon ball. I felt my own heart melting, and feared that I also would fall from my seat. Such an astonishing effect, so sudden and overpowering, I seldom or never saw before. The preacher that day was William McKendree, afterward bishop; a humble, simplehearted, devout soul, who was always careful to make sure that the Holy Spirit of God should supplement in his preaching whatever of natural or acquired ability he might have had.

Time would fail us to tell of Luther, Calvin, Knox, Fox, Whitefield, and Wesley; of Finney also, and of Inskip, MacDonald, Woods, General Booth and Bresee; of Smith and Walker, of Huff and R. T. Williams, of Goodwin and Morrison, of Schurman and Reynolds, of Carradine also, and Bud Robinson, and H. C. Morrison, and of the myriads whose names are familiar, who in the power of the Spirit preached the saving gospel, and whose works do follow them as evidences that their labors were not in vain in the Lord.

All these were men of high human ability and attainments, but, what is more, they were

Holy Ghost anointed preachers sent forth to make men know and feel the truth of sin and the Savior from it. And their examples are not to us tombs to be garnished, but patterns to be imitated in all that is essential in a Pentecostal ministry. Under them, the gospel came to us "not in word only [although, thank God, it did come in the words of sound doctrine and Bible truth], but also in power, and in the Holy Ghost, and in much assurance." And may we, to whom they passed their torches when they had finished their portion of the course, burn as they burned, run as they ran, and preach as they preached to the glory of God the Father, and of the Son, and of the Holy Ghost! Amen.

4

Effective Preaching Defined

There are two passages in the Epistles of Paul that, taken together, pretty well define the purpose of preaching, and give us a rule by which to measure true success in the holy calling. The first passage is in Rom. 10:12-15 and reads as follows:

> For there is no difference between the Jew and the Greek: for the same Lord over all is rich unto all that call upon him. For whosoever shall call upon the name of the Lord shall be saved. How then shall they call on him in whom they have not believed? and how shall they believe in him of whom they have not heard? and how shall they hear without a preacher? and how shall they hear without a preacher? and how shall they preach, except they be sent, as it is written, How beautiful are the feet of them that preach the gospel of peace, and bring good tidings of good things?

The other passage is in Eph. 4:8-16 and reads as follows:

> Wherefore he saith, When he ascended up on high, he led captivity captive, and gave gifts unto men. And he gave some, apostles; and some, prophets; and some, evangelists; and some, pastors and teachers; for the perfecting of the saints, for the work of the ministry, for the edifying of the body of Christ; till we all come in the unity of the faith, and of the knowledge of the Son of God, unto a perfect man, unto the measure of the stature of the fulness of Christ: that we henceforth be no more children, tossed to and fro, and carried about with every wind of doctrine, by the sleight of men, and cunning craftiness, whereby they lie in wait to deceive; but speaking the truth in love, may grow up into him in all things, which is the head, even Christ: from whom the whole body fitly joined together and compacted by that which every joint supplieth, according to the effectual working in the measure of every part, maketh increase of the body unto the edifying of itself in love.

The *Manual* of the Church of the Nazarene sums this up in a sentence in these words: "Saints will be edified and sinners converted through his ministry." There are really three discernible distinctions in the task to be done by New Testament preachers. These are: (1) to lead the lost to Christ for salvation, (2) to inform and indoctrinate those who have become children of God, and (3) to inspire and direct the church in faith, unity, and good works. This threefold task involves the three discernible orders of the ministry: evangelists, teachers, and pastors.

Dr. G. Campbell Morgan, in his book on *Preaching*, says that there are 8 or 10 Greek words in the New Testament "that refer to the exercise of speech for the impartation of truth"; but he says there are two which are supreme, the others being incidental, though valuable. The two supreme words are *euaggelizo*, which is translated by our phrase "preach the gospel"; and the other is *kerusso*, meaning really a proclamation from a throne, and describes a message as being delivered on behalf of a ruler. Merging the two ideas, Dr. Morgan comes up with the definition: "Preaching is the declaration of the grace of God to human need on the authority of the Throne of God; and it demands on the part of those who hear that they show obedience to the thing declared."

Dr. Morgan goes on to say that when the preacher addresses a crowd, he should always remember that his object is the human will. He may approach along the line of the emotions, but he is after the will. He may approach along the line of the intellect, but still he is after the will, and his preaching is successful only when he influences the will. The preacher brings good news, but he brings it from the King, and his message is not to be trifled with. Men have not done enough when they have acknowledged changed feelings or convinced judgment—they must be changed in will to be truly changed.

Dr. Morgan then gave as his estimate:

> We are facing today the biggest hour the world has known for preaching. The miseries

> of theological controversy that are blighting our age cannot satisfy. The mass of men are waiting for preaching of the New Testament kind, with a great message of grace to meet human need, delivered by men who realize that they represent a Throne, and have the right to claim submission to it.

In his approach to the sacred task of preaching, the preacher should come deeply conscious that all the sins, sorrows, and perplexities of the human race are the background for this work. And he should come in the full knowledge and consciousness that he has from God a message of good tidings "for all people." He must come with the conviction that he has here, in the gospel he is to preach, an answer to the world's perplexities, and a cure for its deep diseases.

He should come fully conscious of his own limitations, but, as the prophet of the Lord, he should speak his message boldly and without in any way blurring its contents. His task is not so much to explain the message as to proclaim it. The gospel of Christ is reasonable, so long as it is within the sphere of reason. It is never unreasonable, but it does, at reason's limits, pass on into the sphere of the miraculous. It is not the preacher's task to bring the gospel down to where adepts of reason can define and defend it; it is his task to extol its glorious power unto salvation.

Jefferson, in *The Minister as Prophet*, says:

> The work of preaching is the most difficult of all the things which a minister is called to do. . . . The greatest danger confronting the

> Church of Christ in America today is a possible decadence of the pulpit. . . . So long as Luther and Calvin and Latimer and Knox, and the mighty men who came after them, kept the pulpit fires burning, the world rolled more and more into light, and it was daybreak everywhere. But when the preachers slid down into pedants, there was darkness once more on the earth. . . .
>
> England in the eighteenth century was dead, and it was a preacher—John Wesley—who raised the dead and ushered in a new epoch of Christian history. Has not America had the same experience? Did we not start with Cotton and Hooker and Shepard and Eliot and the Mathers, and did not people who sat in the shadow of great hardships see a wonderful light? And when the light faded, it was because the great preachers were dead; and there was no life and no light in New England till an Englishman, George Whitefield, and an American, Jonathan Edwards, stood in the pulpit, like anointed princes of God, and spoke once more to the people, in burning accents, the message of redemption. The bones in the valley of death have always taken to themselves flesh and stood erect on their feet, and the water has always gushed out of the rock, and new heavens have always bent over a new earth whenever and whereever a man has appeared who was able to convert the pulpit into a throne.

We must have preachers. The Church must have preachers. The community must have preachers. The nations must have preachers. There is a dearth of preachers, even considered from the approach of numbers. There may be overchurched communities where there are more preachers than are altogether needed, but there are also many communities that have no preacher of any sort. The dearth of effective preachers is greater than can be estimated.

The age demands men of power. It demands men who themselves enjoy a deep and rich religious experience; who have heeded a clear and urgent call, a call from God, to preach; who have paid the price or are now willing to pay the price for a thorough preparation; who possess the true shepherd heart; and who have the grace and ability to preach. These five essentials, in the judgment of Bishop Boaz as presented in his book *The Essentials of Effective Preaching*, are indispensable if the Church and the ministry are to hold their own, much less to make consistent gains, in this day and age of the world.

Jefferson puts it strongly thus:

> Unless we can get men for the pulpit as brainy and competent, as versatile and resourceful, as virile and effective, as the great captains of industry and the merchant princes, the church will be handicapped in her labor and the ungodly will have fresh occasion to blaspheme. Bunglers in language and blunderbusses in the art of thinking cannot expect to catch and hold the attention of the rising generation.

I feel now that I must copy the method of the writer to the Hebrews and interject an exhortation. I call upon you, young men and young women, whatever else you may want to do, set as your first decision that you will be preachers. Give yourselves wholly to this ideal. Pay the price for success in this work. Do not be content to be ministers by vocation—be a preacher by calling, and use that saying "Woe is me if I preach not the gospel!" to mean that you will feel disgraced if you do not make good preachers of the glorious gospel you have been commissioned to proclaim. Feel that you have no right to disgrace the pulpit with sermons that make no impression and accomplish nothing.

If you are poor preachers, you make it hard for other preachers, and you bring the pulpit into disrepute. Men and women judge Christianity by preachers and preaching; and if your preaching is shallow and dull, the impression is that the religion you profess is also shallow and dull. You claim to proclaim Christ, and if your preaching is unattractive, men will think Christ is like your preaching. There is no way to estimate the damage a poor preacher can do. And in spite of the many defenses and the partial compensations, the church has no attractions that can atone for a poor preacher. Men may rant and scream and make big claims, but "it has pleased God through the foolishness of preaching [not through foolish preaching] to save them that believe."

It counts for nothing that we offer the alibi of an indifferent age in which preachers are not held in high esteem. What of it, if it is thus? So much the more is it our obligation to make the fire so hot that indifference will melt away, and serve the pulpit so well that it will deserve to be esteemed. Yours is indeed a difficult calling, but who would want a calling that is not difficult? At least we can all rejoice that we are in a line of noble succession. Think of the pulpit giants that have preceded us. Thomas Goodwin, an old Puritan preacher, said, "God had only one Son, and He made Him a minister."

Speaking of "preaching ability," Bishop Boaz names as the natural groundwork "a sound body, a good voice, and a bright mind." Following these, the bishop lists "knowledge," "skill," and "personality." He admits that many must labor against handicaps in the items included in the first triad: we know there have been effective preachers who labored always in physical weakness and even in pain; some, like Jonathan Edwards, have had to contend with weak voices; and many have to fight against intellectual limitations. But even with these admissions, it is well that we should none of us overlook these matters as though they were of small consequence.

Have the will to be well, and be willing to live so that your body will serve to the limits of its possibilities. Henry Ward Beecher said the soul is like a cannon, the body like a cannon carriage, and it is impossible to maneuver the cannon without a well-adapted carriage. The voice is to the preacher what the right arm is to the blacksmith, and the wise preacher will take care of his voice, and do whatever he can to develop and train it. No one can be a good preacher unless he can train himself to think clearly and quickly, and unless he can train himself to imagine vividly, for, as Dr. Talmage used to say, no preacher can hold an audience unless he can either tell stories or paint pictures.

On Bishop Boaz' second triad—knowledge, skill, and personality—it is in the history of Christianity that our holy faith has been promoted by just three general methods: (1) miracles, (2) influence or example, and (3) doctrine. But to preach doctrine, a preacher must know his Bible and know Christian doctrine, and he will need to know as much as he can of nature and of men. D. L. Moody said, "I will not read any book if it will not help me to understand the Book—the Bible." But one cannot always know what purpose a book will serve until he reads it, for one cannot depend on the advice of others.

Books, like friends, are personal companions, and what will help one person will not help everyone. Cicero said, "An orator should know everything." This is a big order, but it represents the ideal, not the actual and the real, for anyone. But at least the preacher must know that he is to preach, and he must be able to say what he knows in a pleasing and effective manner. The subject of personality is indeed a difficult one, but I thing no one is likely to do better with it than did Bishop Boaz himself. He said:

> By personality I mean the sum total of his life and character. A great preacher must live a great life. Before preaching well he must live well. A preacher with a small soul, a narrow vision, and a selfish aim cannot possibly preach a great sermon. The preacher that does

> not struggle with strong endeavor to live the gospel that he preaches cannot reach the highest efficiency. . . . The sermon consists of the truth that is uttered plus the personality of the preacher.
>
> Dr. George A. Buttrick says, concerning the preacher and his sermon, "Physical vitality is a factor. It gives red blood to a sermon and infects listeners with health and cheer. Mental keenness is also a factor. A sharp intellectual scythe is better in time of harvest than a dull blade. But the purity of a man's motive outweighs all other elements in his influence and almost cancels out all other factors" (quoted from *Jesus Came Preaching*).

Bishop Boaz adds as the seventh requisite to effective preaching "the presence and power of the Holy Spirit." This has been the divine plan always. In whatever other things effective preachers may differ, in this one thing they are all alike, for no one can preach the Spirit's message except the Spirit empower him.

And now, returning to the definition of effective preaching with which we started, we present the three implications of that definition in a little further detail, and in summary.

What Effective Preaching Involves

1. Winning men to God

Paul called on Timothy to "do the work of an evangelist." This was not necessarily an order for Timothy to leave his pastorate at Ephesus and become a traveling evangelist.

Rather it was a challenge to him to win souls right where he was.

Our tendency to see parts as though they were the whole has led us to suppose a conflict between "personal evangelism" and "mass evangelism." But the fact is these two forms of soul winning have always been complementary and inseparable. There have been no examples of successful mass evangelism in which personal evangelism did not play a very large and indispensable part, and personal evangelism unattached from gospel preaching has been altogether disappointing. The two go together. It is not within our present scope to speak at length of personal evangelism, except to commend it as the historic practice, and the indispensable adjunct of any and all successful methods of bringing sinners to Christ.

But taking it as the assumption, that all other methods of getting results in definite conversions are approved and enjoined, the preacher should preach to bring men to decision, to prayer, to repentance, and to faith for salvation. A London minister once complained to Spurgeon that he had no conversions in his meetings. Spurgeon asked, "Do you plan for conversions and expect conversions?" The minister had to admit that he did not, although he said he very much wished that conversions might take place. Spurgeon replied that he planned to have conversions in his meetings, expected to have them, and did have them.

We are not here dealing with methods. There are some ministers who plan to have conversions right along in the regular and special services of the church. There are some who plan to make the regular meetings seed sowing, and wait for the special revival effort to actually stress immediate decisions. Both these methods have been followed successfully. Our thought is not to posit a method, but to insist that whatever the method, go in to make it work. Plan to have souls and expect to have souls. This is one of the tests of effective preaching.

No one should judge a preacher hastily. It takes longer to get results sometimes and in some places than at other times and in other places. But, with due regard for the time element, the preacher should expect souls to be saved as a result of his preaching. There are times and places where an altar call is out of place; and too much urging for a forward movement when the atmosphere is not right may result in hardening and in harm. The preacher must use wisdom, and he should not be criticized hastily or unduly urged to do what is against his judgment. But, with all these things taken into consideration, the preacher should demand souls as his hire. God has promised to enable him to "catch men," and he should set himself to the task of catching them and should not give up until he does catch them.

The true Church is composed of "born again" people, and the Church will disappear with the death of its present members if we do not matriculate from the world of the unsaved.

Our own children are in need of definite conversion; our neighbors and our neighbors' children are in need of salvation; every person in the community and in the world is lost without Christ. We have the only method there is—that of preaching the gospel—for saving men from sin and from hell; let us use this means and expect God to bless it and give us definite fruit. Preacher, no matter what other phase of ministerial labor may fall to your lot, "make full proof of your ministry" by doing the work of an evangelist.

2. Establishing God's people in the doctrines of the gospel

This is the work of the teacher. And yet it was to the same preacher that he later told to do the work of an evangelist that Paul said, "Take heed unto thyself, and unto the doctrine; continue in them, for in doing this thou shalt both save thyself, and them that hear thee" (1 Tim. 4:16). The evangelist needs doctrine as well as miracles and influence, and the preacher who would establish the people of God so that they will not be "tossed about" by heresies, must deliberately and consistently indoctrinate them. It is of little use for the average preacher to fight heresies directly, for heresies have a way of flourishing on opposition. The preacher's task is to get there first with more than the others can ever bring. He must get there before the cultists and the heretics arrive, and he must fill the storehouse of his hearers minds so full of "the truth as it is in Christ Jesus" that when these others come, there will be no room for them or for their wares.

Apostolic Christianity has always been dogmatic, and it is bound always to be so. The reply of the apostolic preacher to those who would bid him either hold his peace or preach something liberal is "We can but speak the things we have seen and heard." No preacher is a prophet who says, "If there is a God," "If Christ is divine," "If man is a sinner," "If the Holy Spirit is a person," "If salvation is a fact," "If all men must die and appear before God in judgment," "If there is eternal destiny awaiting us all." These are verities which admit of no compromise and of no uncertainty. Philosophers may speculate about these things, but preachers must preach them, as men "having authority." Scientists may arise to say they have not found inbred sin in the laboratory or seen the Star of Bethlehem in the literal skies, but preachers must stand up to announce the revelation of God concerning sin and the Saviour from it.

Indoctrination is more than an intellectual process. Men need to be told and retold what they already know or are supposed to know. That is why "those who know it best, seem hungering and thirsting" to hear the old, old story of Christ and salvation like those who are hearing it for the first time. Many preachers are deceived by their own impression that "these people know this truth and will not be benefited by having it rehearsed." They may know it, and yet it may not be vivid with them.

And besides that, men need to be told again the very things they know, for truth has a tendency to become static and ineffective if allowed to rest too long.

There is need, I think, of a word of warning regarding books, papers, and sermons which appear these days in printed form. Many of these are good and useful; but too many of them are obtuse and, if read exclusively or excessively, tend to affect the preacher's style and make him obtuse. Of course we must use tact, but the line separating tact and compromise is narrow at times, and we need to watch that we do not round our corners until the diamond of truth ceases to have cutting edges. The effective preacher will habitually choose great themes. Themes like The Atonement, Sin (actual and inbred), Man's Lost Estate, The Deity of Jesus Christ, The Personality and Office Work of the Holy Spirit, Repentance, The New Birth, The Witness of the Spirit, Consecration, Entire Sanctification, Holiness of Heart and Life, The Second Coming of Christ, The Resurrection of the Dead, The Final Judgment, Hell, Heaven, and The Immortality of the Soul. These are just the great wide themes, and the preacher must needs present them repeatedly, in parts and in full. Let no man's presence deter the preacher's determination to have an intelligent, as well as a spiritual church; for if the people are truly good, they need the protection of indoctrination to keep them so, and good people love doctrine—that is, good people who are also wise people.

Right from our own holiness churches come complaints that holiness is not much preached. The suggestion is not that the preacher does not believe in holiness nor that the person complaining does not believe in it or understand it. The complaint is based on the ground that "when the pulpit is silent long on a theme, the pew ceases to believe," and there is ground for this fear. When preachers preach on any doctrine seldom or with slight emphasis, the listeners must of necessity gather that that doctrine is not very important.

Forty years ago in our holiness associations we were told that the test of a holiness preacher is his ability to preach doctrine and get blessed and bless others while doing so. The idea, prevalent in some church circles, that doctrinal preaching is dry and uninteresting is a false idea, if it is intended to say that it is so of necessity. No doubt it is true in many cases; but when this is true of doctrinal preaching, it is probably true in a large measure where that preacher preaches, regardless of the type of sermon offered.

But mere loyalty to the program is not enough. A preacher can preach on worthy themes like the old Scottish preacher preached his 12 sermons on "The Existence of God." At the close of the series, the preacher asked an old deacon what he thought of the sermons. The honest old layman replied, "Well, milord, I must say that after hearing all you have had to say on the subject, I still believe there is a God."

The preacher, to preach doctrine successfully, must be "full of his subject." He must know his doctrine thoroughly. He must study to present the doctrines interestingly and instructively. He must give out enough of the familiar to keep his informed hearers sure that he is orthodox and on the right track. Then he must present enough that is new that the informed will be better informed when he is through. This is in line with the observation of Jesus that "every scribe which is instructed unto the kingdom of heaven is like unto a man that is an householder, which bringeth forth out of his treasure things new and old" (Matt. 13:52). The old is the guarantee of orthodoxy, and the new is the element of freshness; and to preach an old doctrine so that it is challenging and interesting is the test of a good preacher in a movement that majors on doctrine.

Our church, and the churches of our group, do not profess to base church membership on the minimum of either light or practice. We admit that one might be a Christian and not believe, not having heard, many things which are involved in our brief statement of doctrine given out at the time of the reception of members. We also admit that men may be Christians and still practice some things which we prohibit, and not live up to some things which we enjoin. We cannot there fall back on the easy way of saying, "Oh, if he is truly right with God, God will show him." God will indeed show him all that is essential to his life and usefulness, but he will use the preacher as an instrument in showing him these things.

We do not share the easy way of those who say, "No matter what you believe, just so you are honest in it." For while we know that many men are better than their doctrine, just as many are not so good as their doctrine would require, yet the advantage of sound doctrine has the force of apostolic judgment and authority for its claim. To "preach the word" means to preach the doctrines the Word proclaims—merely reciting memorized scriptures is not preaching, even though it may be done to advantage in connection with preaching, and even though it is a worthy exercise when altogether detached.

3. Inspiring and directing the church in faith, unity, and good works

There is nothing in which Paul exercises greater patience and persistence than in his counsels to be of good courage, and his exhortations to be united and busy in the work of God. He exhorted Christians to present their bodies a living sacrifice to God as a "reasonable service"; asked them to "forgive one another," even as Christ had forgiven them; pled with them to "keep the unity of the Spirit in the bonds of peace"; likened the Church to the human body in which every member is affected by the plight or pleasure of every other member; and concluded his peerless discourse on the resurrection with the challenging call: "Therefore, my beloved brethren, be ye stedfast, unmoveable, always abounding in the work of the Lord, for as much as ye know that your labour is not in vain in the Lord."

The Greeks had the saying: "Whom the gods would destroy, they first make angry." I would paraphrase this for ourselves by saying, "Whom the devil would defeat, he first divides." There is, of course, a cheap substitute for unity based upon union of front, even a uniformity of name and method, which can be attained by mere human manipulations and agreements. But true unity is a thing of the spirit and makes demands that go deeper than the simple "agree to disagree" that is so often eulogized, or even than that "compromise for the sake of peace" which has been recommended as a healing for the factions in the Christian world. The preacher is but skimming the surface when he says, "Let's get together on this matter"; for while that is sufficient when nothing more than methods are involved, it is "healing the afflictions of the daughter of my people slightly" when carnality and selfishness rise up to disturb.

There are afflictions in the church that are like a rash on the skin that can be healed by the application of salves and ointments. But there are other afflictions that are like a cancer in the liver that can be healed only by fundamental medicine or major surgery. For these latter ailments the gospel of the saving and sanctifying grace of Christ is essential, and the truth must be spoken in love and in the power of the Spirit to bring about the fundamental amends that are implied. A truly spiritual church is a united church, so the motive of the preacher centers on the means of securing and maintaining a spiritual church, with the full knowledge that unity and agressiveness will then follow.

Faith, in the sense of attitude, means to be courageous. There is no denying that the Christian way is a way of battle; but normally, it is also a way of victory in the battle, after the battle, and at the end of the way. It is impossible to estimate the trouble and the woe that faces the preacher every time he stands up before an audience. Many people cover the signs of their sorrow so effectively that even their intimates know little of their inner sufferings. But it is the preacher's privilege to help his people "bury their sorrows in the bosom of the Man of Sorrows," and turn again to smile and to extol the wonders of grace. The cult that has for its creed "Health, Happiness, and Prosperity" has a catchy motto, but it can have a limited clientele; for there are many who are sick, unhappy, and poor, and to these the true preacher of Christ is sent to tell them of holiness and joy and everlasting life which are the antitypes of these earthly goods that have been denied them.

There is a thesis which I have named "The Doctrine of Christian Triumphant," which is at the very hub of the Christian belief; and by it men are taught that "sorrow and weeping may endure for the night, but joy cometh in the morning," and that nothing ultimately bad can come to one who truly walks with God. Like the fire of Nebuchadnezzar's furnace, the heat of earth's trials may serve to burn off the bindings of the saint; but it is powerless to scorch the saint himself, and in the end he shall come out in light and life and everlasting victory. This is the preacher's message to those who are weary and heavy laden, to the burdened and distressed, to the bruised and suffering among the people of God.

It is often difficult to distinguish between being saved by good works and being saved to good works; so that one thinks it is the merits of his works that will bring him to heaven; and the other, knowing he is saved by unmerited grace, wants to begin to rest and wear his crown right now instead of working and bearing his cross. But to the preacher is given the blessed task of inspiring his people to be good and do good for the love of Jesus' sake, and to keep them "looking unto Jesus" for salvation, while yet working with their eyes on the recompence of the reward which awaits them when they reach heaven, "saved by grace."

We may not know what form reward in heaven will take. All we ever hear of this matter must of necessity be couched in the language of earth, and such a vehicle is unsuited to bear the burden of heavenly values. Our hearts instinctively respond to the sentiment, "Just to be there and to look on His face, Oh, that will be glory for me!" And yet, it may be that in heaven we would welcome another day on earth that we might do something we neglected while we had the chance. At any rate, we are confident that while we shall have all eternity to shout over victories won, we have only our time here on earth to win those victories.

Ramis Horn Brown once had a cartoon in his paper which represented the preacher as hitched up and pulling a wagon, while the majority of the church members rode on the wagon, some even dragging their feet. This picture is undoubtedly true to life as life appears in many churches. And the preacher is often to blame. He is to blame not only because he thinks nothing is done well unless he does it himself, but because he has not preached effectively in inspiring the people to obey the inner inspiration to "undertake great things for God and expect great things from God." D. L. Moody said, "It is better to put 10 men to work than to do 10 men's work." It is better to inspire a church to work for God than to do the work the church is set to do. An active church is usually a united and a happy church. Indifference is both a cause and an effect of inactivity.

Now is summing up our definition of effective preaching: Preaching is effective when the preacher does the work of an evangelist, the work of a teacher, and the work of a shepherd; when he wins souls, indoctrinates the Christians, and unites the church in worship and service. That most preachers have qualities that savor of one or two of these forms of service, and that few are equally good at all, no one will question. But no one can truly say that it is enough that a preacher should be confined to only one of these offices. If a preacher finds his talents run largely toward one or the other of these forms of ministry, he does well to think of this as a providence suggesting his greatest field of usefulness. But he is unwise if he surrounds himself with the idea that only that one form of service is important, and that the world would be better off if all preachers were such as he. He is also unwise if he decides that he can neglect for himself all other forms than the one in which he can find the largest joy and the widest apparent success. Take Paul for an example: the missionaries say Paul was the first and the greatest foreign missionary; the evangelists think of him as the founder of new churches and preacher at large in the field of evangelism; but pastors use Paul for their pattern, too; and Paul himself claimed his effort was to "be all things to all men, that I might by all means win some."

But whatever the form of evidence, let none of us think that God called us to the ministry designing that we shall fail in it. The very fact that He called you is evidence that you could succeed as a preacher; as to whether you will succeed or not, only you can determine that. There may be callings in which a defeatist can serve successfully; if so, the task of preaching is not one of them. The truly effective preacher must go forth like the rider of the white horse, "conquering and to conquer."

Some soil is more difficult to cultivate, and hence the harvest there is slower than in other places; but let us take our appointments as being made in heaven, no matter by what channel they may be brought to us, and let us, in spite of adverse wind or weather, "sow beside all waters," and let us then claim for our own that special promise to preachers and to soul winners: "He that goeth forth and weepeth, bearing precious seed, shall doubtless come again with rejoicing, bringing his sheaves with him" (Ps. 126:6).

5

The Practice of Preaching Illustrated

Ruskin, lecturing in London on the subject of art, came to examples and said, "I will name just one," and gave the name of Michelangelo. That is the way I feel like doing in coming to this last lecture on "The Preaching Ministry." I am to illustrate preaching in this division, and, of course, I must do so by the study of examples. But in the true sense there is but one example, and that is the Lord Jesus Christ himself. It were enough for me to say, "Look at Him, and then go and do it as He did it." And if you will do this, I shall be content, and shall think you wiser in your choice than though you went with me down the picture gallery of preaching men and preaching women in all the years that have followed since that Man of Galilee preached on the mountaintops, on the seashore, in the synagogues, on the campus of the Temple, in the homes, on the roadsides, and in the fields of Galilee, Perea, and Judea.

No matter what secondary patterns we may name, let it be forever understood that they are of value only as they serve to give a little close up study of the Master Pattern in whom all the excellencies of the preaching art have their spring and center. Jesus, as a preacher, is like the whole visible sky above our heads; the examples we shall cite in illustrations are like just that little spot in the celestial universe which the astronomer studies through his focused telescope; and if our examples are in anything unlike Him, it is because they do not reflect the light, for He is the fullness of excellencies in this, as in every other phase and calling of life, both now and in the world to come.

Chronology is the very easiest string there is for tying together the incidents which make up experience and life. This is why people who do not keep written records so accurately remember that certain things happened when a certain child was young, and why they must be allowed to tell many incidental and unimportant things in order that they may recall accurately the matter about which they are asked. It is the mark of an educated person to be able to give an occurrence without giving its pedigree or its environment. Nevertheless, in this chapter on "The Practice of Preaching Illustrated," I am going to use chronology as my principle of guidance in the organization of the matter in hand.

1. The Preacher's Beginnings

I shall pass over the preacher's birth and his irresponsible years, because these, though of tremendous importance in his making, are altogether in the hands of God and of others than the preacher himself. Enough for us to believe and know that we were in God's care, even in the days when we knew not how to care for ourselves or how even to be appreciative of the care of mothers. Even as it was with Jeremiah, God chose us for the ministry and elected to for us the parentage, the home, and the early surroundings which became our capital at the time when we were ready to take over as responsible agents.

We begin with conversion and the beginnings of distinctive Christian consciousness. The person designed to be the prophet of the Lord will undoubtedly be conscious of God's definite dealings with his soul. No one whose own religious experience was and is hazy will be a clear and definite preacher. We would not posit knowledge of time and place as of preeminent importance; but conversion, like the natural birth to which it was likened by our Lord, is certainly a breaking forth into the light; and if one, even though he be young and tender at the time, has been really convicted for sin by the Spirit of God, will have a definite sense of relief from jeopardy when the sense of pardon comes; and even to a little child, the witness of the Spirit to adoption and sonship may be clear and above doubt.

The earlier one can know of the experience of entire sanctification, and come to know it as the state and experience of the heart, the better it is. For although the experience of a long, unrequited search may engender patience in dealing with others in a like state, it cannot atone for the loss of time and the stunt of growth that result from living only in the twilight of the Pentecostal day. What is more, the preacher's great business in the days of his power will not be to tell people how not to get the blessing, but how to really receive it.

His best work will not be done on old, chronic doubters, but on young people and children, with whom faith is more normal than doubt. But the principal demand is for a sound and knowable experience when it does appear; for no preacher of uncertain experience in the grace of holiness can be trusted to preach this gospel faithfully and efficiently to others. Among those we have known who, after a time of apparent devotion, turned aside from preaching holiness to "another gospel," one of the principal causes for the change was, in the background, an unsatisfactory experience in the preacher's own heart. Wesley found in his day that preachers will not long faithfully preach perfect love to others after they have ceased to enjoy the blessing themselves.

God has a way of making His will known to His children; and the call to preach is indicated to each individual in a characteristic manner. God, in such cases, simply speaks the individual language of His child. But always the fact is made clear enough to enable the true prophet to rest upon the abiding conviction that God has designed him for this service. This conviction is sufficient to hold the preacher steady amidst many storms and in the midst of "fightings without and fears within" through which, during the days of his labors, he is bound to be called upon to pass. The call to preach is an honor, when it comes; but it is not to be sought and is not to be presumed. It is to be taken, when given, with both trembling and rejoicing. The trembling is indicative of the responsibility involved, and the rejoicing is indicative of a sense of the honor bestowed.

A call to preach is, with any person, a call to prepare to preach. If the call comes early, it is a call to go to school—to complete the grades, the high school, and the college. And in these days no young preacher who finds education possible should be content even with college but should bend his energies to get seminary training. This full course of preparation is a question for doubt, as I believe, only with those who are not fully cognizant of the demands made upon the preacher of today and tomorrow. The preacher needs all that the schools can do for him. He needs it, and the church needs it in him. And it is better that he should take time to get ready, as far as this is possible, before he enters into the ministry as a vocation. He should preach, as opportunity offers, any time and every time along the way, from the day he is conscious of his designation for the task; but he can save his own time and the time of the people he is elected to serve if he can concentrate on preparation before he becomes too involved with family and ecclesiastical responsibilities.

There have always been provisions in the program of a Pentecostal movement for the exceptional preacher and for the preacher to whom the call comes at a period so late in life as to preclude formal education. But these exceptional preachers can do their work better if those who can, will make full preparation for their work. An uneducated preacher can do better service in a church or movement where his want of learning is the exception than he can in a setup where education is at a discount, and culture is confused with pretense.

Contrary to the popular thought on the subject, educated preachers have set the standard for sacrifice and unselfish service, and have themselves been the principle examples of such. In the course of true education, one learns to discount so many things that true values are more normal at the end than at the beginning. I have not the slightest fear about the graduates of our seminary as regards their willingness to accept poor charges in small churches at home and hard, labor-demanding appointments in our foreign fields. Those who think and say otherwise are uninformed as regarding both the content and the effect of education, and they are unaware of what the history of Christianity shows.

So I repeat, it has been educated preachers who have done the exacting labor that requires self-forgetfulness, as names like Paul, Athanasius, Augustine, Luther, Wesley, Finney, and that host whose graves are in heathen lands where they went in search of souls do testify. We welcome those whose circumstances make formal education unavailable, but we urge all those with whom such a course is possible to take advantage of all the schools, colleges, and seminary can do for them in preparing them for the most blessed and the most difficult task ever assigned to mortal men.

2. The Preacher's Opportunities

The question How shall I get started? has confronted many a young preacher and all but frustrated him. But, like many other troubles, this one usually looks worse from a distance than it does when it is seen at close approach. Someone will take an interest in the young preacher. Someone will want to hear him preach. Someone will become burdened for him and want to see him have a chance. Church leaders, both lay and clerical, are always scouting for prospective preachers. Our people are quite loyal in carrying out the exhortation of our *Manual*, "When the church discovers this divine call, the proper steps should be taken for its recognition and endorsement, and all suitable help should be given to open the way into the ministry."

Speaking now from experience, as well as from observation, I think it is a good thing for the beginning preacher to let the responsibility for his invitations rest with others. If those responsible ask him to preach, he should accept and do his best; for while the hearers may not receive immediate benefit, we learn to preach by preaching, and in the interest of those who shall hear us later on, we should use our opportunities for practice. And, more still on the same line, I believe we should always use whatever opportunity is present, and wait for that "better opportunity" while busy, rather than wait for it with folded hands.

Dr. L. T. Corlett once wrote me that he was leaving his pastorate and that he would consider a new location. I was interested and began casting about. But soon the word came that he had accepted a small church with limited opportunity. When I saw him, I asked why he was so hasty. His answer was "My father told me never to be out of a job. I was about to leave the pastorate I was in, and I thought it better to leave it to go somewhere than to leave it to go nowhere." And looking back now from this distance, it is clear, I think, that he was much wiser than are those preachers, young or experienced, who sit in unemployment and ask for calls. Everybody prefers a busy man to an idle one, and the Scriptures favor the idea that even God takes a busy man for His work rather than one who is not in demand by anyone.

I have seen preachers who integrity I did not doubt, but whose wisdom I felt free to criticize, who would pass up present opportunities which they considered unpromising to wait for "something with an opportunity." I have known evangelists to cancel "small meetings" that they might be in position to accept meetings that had a stronger appeal. But I can say that I never did any of these things. I admit that, like Dr. E. F. Walker used to say of himself, I have always been "easy to be intreated" when it comes to preaching; but I have always preached on invitation and have never passed a sincere invitation in the hope that a better might appear. Nor have I ever canceled a meeting in the "sap oaks" to accept a call to a state camp. And in defense of others, I have to say that I have had abundant opportunity and have not often wished for a chance to preach when no such chance was available. I believe God will take care of the opportunity question, and I have been and am yet content to leave this matter in His hands, taking what He gives and doing without what He withholds.

This attitude, I believe, is fundamental if the preacher is always to meet in his own mind and conscience the accusations of men and demons that he is "out of the will of God" and doing what he is doing because he has a pull or because he is moved by ulterior motives. There are no little places or big places in the work of God. His place is the right place, and it is a place you can fill if you fully obey Him. And I know, also by experience, that when one is coming out toward the finish of his day in the Lord's vineyard, it is wonderfully comforting to be able to know and to say, "I have neither sought place nor shunned responsibility."

3. The Preacher's Care

Dr. Jowett, while pastor of Fifth Avenue Presbyterian Church in New York, was of limited physical strength, and determined to confine his preaching and public speaking to his own church. But the fame of his ability brought many invitations. Once an invitation was so pressing that the committee finally said, "Please come. We need you. You need not talk long. If we can announce that you will be there, and you will favor us with a 10-minute talk, we shall be satisfied." Jowett yielded and promised to go. But later that committee was embarrassed, if not horrified, to find that this busy pastor found it necessary to use two full days in preparing that 10-minute address. If any are inclined to think this was too much work for such an address, let him speak only after he has found his addresses as well received and as effective as were Dr. Jowett's. The story but illustrates how seriously one great man took his work. With him it was not that one address that was at stake, but it was his own fidelity to duty and the reputation of the pulpit for which he was responsible.

Having disposed of the question of general preparation in a former division, we here bring up that of specific preparation. The time for preaching is now close at hand. Within a week the preacher will stand before a crowd of men and women to do what he can to meet their need for light and strength and blessings through the divine institution of preaching. What shall the preacher do to get ready?

Well, in the first place, he must prepare himself through prayer, meditation upon God and God's Word, consideration of the people who shall be his hearers, thought upon the occasion and the atmosphere in which he will preach, and in every possible way prepare himself inwardly to meet the demands that are soon to come upon him. His working, sleeping, eating, and recreational habits must all take their plan from the consideration of the preacher as a preacher. He will need to be in physical trim, in mental alertness, in spiritual victory. More fundamental than any other preparation is the preparation of the preacher himself, for it is truth plus the preacher's personality that is preaching.

Then there is the sermon. Timeliness is the principal consideration in the selection of the theme and the subject. The preacher must be directed by an inner voice if he is to be wise in this. The hearers are of more importance than the subject. The preacher may do something to adapt the hearers to the theme, but he must also adapt the theme to the hearers. Having settled on the theme, there is the selection of the text or scripture portion to be used as the basis for the sermon. This should be selected carefully and read repeatedly. If there are proper names in it, these should be pronounced correctly. If there are unfamiliar words, these should be read with proper emphasis that the meaning may come out naturally.

The context must be studied again and again, though it may be for the hundredth time. All the Bible says on the subject should be read and taken into consideration. The subject itself must be made to stand out clearly. Then the divisions of the subject or theme should be made on the basis of simplicity and clarity. Too many divisions are both unnecessary and confusing. The oratorical order as well as the logical order should be considered in the arrangement of the divisions, and the plan must be to conclude on the high peak. The old advice to "begin low, go slow, rise higher, strike fire, and sit down in a storm" is still good for the preacher who is after results.

Illustrations are good but should not be multiplied and should be as fitting as possible. Illustrations that hinge upon questionable morals or doubtful religion should be avoided; people are too likely to take the moral of the story rather than that of the argument which led up to the story. The wide-awake preacher will not want for illustrations, for these are all about us, even as they were all about Jesus in the simple homes and fields and roads of Palestine.

On the question of exact preparation, there is room for adaptation to the preacher's type. But if you plan to be an exact preacher and plan to be a growing preacher, you must write. No preacher should fail to write one full sermon a week during the first 10 years of his ministry, whether he ever preaches that sermon or not. The exercise will be laborious, and the returns will not be immediately apparent; but the preacher's regard for accuracy will be promoted, and in the later days of his work he will have occasion to be thankful for the results of such discipline.

Read sermons are poor listening. If the preacher must write to bring assurance before the crowd, then he better go another step and memorize. Some preachers known for their unctuous preaching, like Seth C. Rees, regularly memorized their sermons and believed they could give more attention to results by not having to be troubled with efforts to recall content. But on this, every preacher must find his own way. It is a rule, I think, that a preacher can train himself to think on his feet, before a crowd, and be as helped by the freshness and aptness of his own thoughts as his hearers are.

4. The Preacher's Effort

We have come now to the crises—to the time when the preacher must preach or miss his opportunity. If the preacher is fortunate, the service of which the sermon is a part is one service, having been planned by one mind, and consciously carried through with a given purpose. If he is not fortunate, there have already been two or three detached services. There may have been "a song service"; if the worst has happened, there has been "a *rousing* song service," the leader having no regard for the preaching but just for a singing service. Perhaps there has been "a prayer service," a "testimony service," and, who knows, "a money-raising service"! And now, as a sort of cracker on the whip, there is to be a preaching service.

If the situation is like this latter by the preacher's own choosing, it is probably an effort, conscious or otherwise, to cover up the fact that there is to be a poor sermon. If it is not of the preacher's choosing, he can get a lot of consolation out of that chimney-corner scripture which says, "Grin and bear it." The atmosphere of the meeting may have been prepared so that all are ready for the sermon, or it may be that the preacher will have to overcome a poor atmosphere either by taking a little time to change it or by rising above it. Anyway, the hour has come. The next few minutes will see how the battle shall go.

A young and successful lawyer, it is said, spent a Sunday with an old college classmate who was a preacher. On Monday the preacher asked the lawyer for his reactions. The lawyer said, "Frankly I was disappointed. In the first place, you did not seem to have your case well in hand. You gave intimations of uncertainty and of uneasiness. You appeared too conscious of what your audience thought about the matter. Then you seemed to want for purpose. You did not press for a decision. You seemed content in the end to let matters go on as they might have gone anyway. You had what we lawyers would call 'a good case,' and I tried to think how I would have handled it. When I take a case, I like to feel that it is a good case. Then I want the subject of the fee settled, and even paid in advance, so that I will not have to think of it anymore. Then I prepare my case with all diligence, quoting precedents, offering arguments, presenting testimony. Then at the end, I press for a decision. I think the jury should see it the way I do, for I think I see it as it is; and I press them to use their judgment and to give me a decision. I am in earnest; I must get results or I feel I have failed my client who has left his interests in my hands."

It is well that the preacher be free from trammels. Preaching "trial sermons" is an experience not to be too often repeated. The sermon must be a real sermon, not just an effort to see if it will do. The preacher should know that few people will feel an obligation to hear him. He must earn his right to be heard, right while others are listening. He has no time to lose. In these days he had better say something during the first five minutes, or it will do little good to say it later along, for by that time the people's minds will be far away. This is a day of quick thinking and of quick interference. The preacher is supposed to be ready the minute he stands up.

The preacher's thoughts must be ready, and his speech must be fluent. He must make every minute count. He must state his thesis plainly; he must make his arguments strong; his language should be correct and his imagery pleasing and impressive. He must not speak in a monotone. He must observe the demands of cadence in a speaking voice. He must end his sentences with strong words, conclude his periods with emphatic sentences, and leave his points sharp. He must make out his case so the ordinary man can understand it. Then the experts may understand it, too.

He must preach what he knows and feels to be true. He must neither speculate nor equivocate. If he has not thought a matter through, he must let it wait. He must preach. People are not interested in his laboratory processes, they want the result of his labors. No one really cares how he came to think of this subject; what all want to know is, What is the truth about it? The preacher cannot hold his audience for lengthy periods with logic along. He must either tell stories or paint pictures or his audience will become surfeited. But he must drive straight ahead. He must keep his goal in sight all the way through, and he must keep his terminal facilities in good repair.

If there are signs of lagging interest, one thing the preacher can do if he has control of himself—he can quit. And if he quits in time, those who did not want him to quit will feel that he was "just getting started," and those who wanted him to quit will think he is smart. But all the way and every time, the preacher is after results. He is more concerned to do justice to his crowd than to his subject—the subject has less feeling and may come again, even if slighted.

All that we have thus far said in this division is like Elijah's altar before the fire came down. The stones are in place, the wood is in order, the sacrifice is upon the wood. But there is no justification for it all unless and until the fire comes down. In his book on *The Tongue of Fire*, William Arthur (pp. 61 and 62):

> Peter was soon called upon publicly to deliver the Lord's message. Then, undoubtedly, he spoke not in any foreign tongue, but in his native dialect. He had often spoken before, yet nothing remarkable is recorded of his preaching, or its effects. He is now the same man, with the same natural intellect, and the same natural powers of speech; and yet a new utterance is given to him, the effects of which are instantly apparent.
>
> Never was such an audience assembled as that before which this poor fisherman appeared: Jews, with all the prejudices of their race—inhabitants of Jerusalem, with the recollection of the part they had recently taken in the crucifixion of Jesus of Nazareth—met in the city of their solemnities, jealous for the honor of their temple and law; men of different nations, rapidly and earnestly speaking in their different tongues: one in the Hebrew, mocking and saying, "These men are full of new wine," another inquiring in Latin; another disputing in Greek; another wondering in Arabic; and an endless babel besides, expressing every variety of surprise, doubt, and curiosity.
>
> Amidst such a scene the fisherman stands up; his voice strikes across the hum which prevails down the street. He has no tongue of silver, for they say, "He is an unlearned and ignorant man." The rudeness of his Galilean speech still remains with him; yet, though "unlearned and ignorant" in their sense—as to polite learning—in a higher sense he was a scribe well instructed. As respected the word of God, he had been for three years under the constant tuition of the prophet of Nazareth, hearing

from his lips instruction in the law, in the prophets, and in all the "deep things of God." On whatever other points, therefore, the learned of Jerusalem might have found Peter at fault, in the sacred writings he was more thoroughly furnished than they; for though Christ took his apostles from among the poor, he left us no example for those who have not well learned the Bible, to attempt to teach it.

Yet Peter had no tongue of silver, no tongue of honey, no soothing, flattering speech, to allay the prejudices and to captivate the passions of the multitude. Nor had he a tongue of thunder; no outbursts of native eloquence distinguished his discourse. Indeed, some, if they had heard that discourse from ordinary lips, would not have hesitated to pronounce it dry—some of a class, too numerous, who do not like preachers who put them to the trouble of thinking, but enjoy only those who regale their fancy, or move their feelings, without requiring any labor of thought.

Peter's sermon is no more than quoting passages from the word of God, and reasoning upon them; yet, as in this strain he proceeds, the tongue of fire by degrees burns its way to the feelings of the multitude. The murmur gradually subsides; the mob becomes a congregation; the voice of the fisherman sweeps from end to end of that multitude, unbroken by a single sound; and as the words rush on, they act like a stream of fire. Now, one coating of prejudice which covered the feelings is burned, and starts aside; now, another and another; now, the fire touches the inmost covering of prejudice, which lay close upon the heart, and it, too, starts aside. Now, it touches the quick, and burns the very soul of the man! Presently, you might think that in the throng there was but one mind, that of the preacher, which had multiplied itself, had possessed itself of thousands of hearts and thousands of frames, and was pouring its own thoughts through them all.

At length, shame, and tears, and sobs overspread that whole assembly. Here, a head bows; there, starts a groan; yonder, rises a deep sigh; here, tears are falling; and some sterm old Jew, who will neither bow nor weep, trembles with the effort to keep himself still. At length, from the depth of the crowd the voice of the preacher is crossed by a cry, as if one was "mourning for his only son"; and is answered by a cry, as if one was in "bitterness for his firstborn." At this cry the whole multitude is carried away; and, forgetful of everything but the overwhelming feeling of the moment, they exclaim: "Men and brethren, what must we do?"

In a later paragraph Dr. Arthur says:

This is the first example of prophesying in the New Testament sense; not the limited sense of foretelling, but the more comprehensive sense of delivering a message from God, under the impulse of the Spirit of God, and by his aid. In this the speaker has the double advantage of ascertained truth to declare—truth which his own understanding has received, which he can enforce by citing the word of God—and of aid direct from the Spirit in uttering it.

In still a later paragraph, Dr. Arthur says:

If the preaching of the gospel is to exercise a great power over mankind, it must be either by enlisting extraordinary men, or by the endowing of ordinary men with extraordinary power. It does often happen that men whose eloquence would affect and sway, whatever might have been their theme, give all their talents to the gospel; yet in such cases it ever proves that the religious impression produced upon mankind is never regulated by the brilliancy or natural force of the eloquence, but always by the extent to which the preacher is imbued with that indescribable something commonly called the "unction," or the operation and power of the Spirit.

On the other hand, it often happens that a man in whose natural gifts nothing extraordinary can be discovered produces moral effects which, for depth at the moment, and for permanency, are totally disproportioned to his natural power. In hearing such a man, and afterwards discovering the effects of his preaching, people often ask: "What is there in Mr.— to account for such effects? We hear many who are abler, profounder, better theologians, more eloquent, more persuasive; yet this man's preaching brings people to repentance and to God." They cannot discover the source of his power; and it is precisely this fact which intimates that it is spiritual.

It is an interesting and helpful study to go on through the Acts of the Apostles looking only for the methods and effects of preaching as they are described therein. There is Stephen, the deacon, whose shining martyr face may have haunted the haughty Saul until he met Jesus on the Damascus road. There is "Philip the evangelist," who pushed out into Samaria and founded a church among the current enemies of Israel. There is Barnabas, whose ministerial qualifications are all set forth in terms of spiritual qualities. There is Timothy, of weak body and strong courage, and Titus, the youth, who was sent back home to be bishop of his kinfolk and countrymen. But they were preachers all, and their number is made the more blessed by the Apostle to the Gentiles, who determined that his preaching should stand in the power of God, and not alone in the logic and philosophy of men. Those were the glorious days of the Church's beginnings, and they were the days when there "were giants in the earth" in the persons of gospel preachers.

Time would fail us to follow the history of preaching and the biographies of preachers down through the centuries when Ambrose preached at Milan, Augustine preached at Carthage, and Chrysostom of the golden mouth sounded forth in St. Sophia at Constantinople. Nor may we listen in on Huss of Bohemia, Savonarola of Florence, or Luther in Germany, though these all shook the earth with quakings more powerful than those which destroyed Pompeii and Herculaneum. Then Calvin in Geneva, Knox in Edinburgh, and Fox and Bunyan and Wesley and the Methodists in England all sounded the trumpet in the ears of their contemporaries. And such men as Ridley and Latimer started fires that, please God, shall never be quenched. Closer to our own times we have had Finney and Spurgeon, Talmage and Beecher, and a great company who made the pulpit a throne and changed the course of nations.

Nor has our own movement wanted for patterns worthy to be followed. There have been Inskip, MacDonald, Wood, Smith, Huff, Carradine, Rees, and Morrison who stood out like high peaks in a mountain range of masters of the pulpit in the interdenominational holiness movement. And in our own church we have had Bresee, Walker, and Williams, a trio which would sit in the one short front row of preachers of the first half-century of our history. Their methods and the effect of their preaching is still so close to our day that I forebear to make estimates. But our heritage is rich for these and others who have wrought among us as masters of the preaching art.

And now, in setting before you some things which I feel are involved in the demand for effective service in "The Preaching Ministry," I have kept in mind always that you must fight to keep the balance between the real and the ideal, so that you will neither be discouraged by your limitations nor come to account any "best" good enough. "A man's reach should exceed his grasp, or what's a heaven for?" If there is not a better preacher beckoning you on, you are already as good a preacher as you will ever be. And if the measure set up sometimes makes us cry, "Who is sufficient for these things?" let our answer be "Our sufficiency is of God; who also hath made us able ministers of the new testament; not of the letter, but of spirit; for the letter killeth, but the spirit giveth life."

I pray for you, and for any to whom these words may come, I pray that you may always possess that divine discontent that will make you noncomplacent in the best day you shall ever see as a preacher of a gospel so glorious that those who have laid down their lives for its propagation have considered themselves fortunate. I pray, too, that there may be given unto you such a blessed measure of the spirit of prophecy and of power that you may be worthy sons of those worthy sires who have made the name of the Christian ministry to be both revered and feared. May you come with good news from the throne of the King, and thus may your message be in grace and in authority and power. And at the crowning day, may you, the undershepherds of God's flock, receive the "well done" of the Chief Shepherd, into whose presence you shall bring the lambs He has entrusted to your care!